I0893898

A Sporting Life

The Memoirs of a Big-Game Hunter

A Sporting Life

The Memoirs of a Big-Game Hunter

by

José A. Martínez de Hoz

Safari Press Inc.

A Sporting Life ©2005 by José A. Martínez de Hoz. All rights reserved. No part of this publication may be used or reproduced in any form or by any means, electronic or mechanical reproduction, including photocopying, recording, or any information storage and retrieval system, without permission from the publisher.

The trademark Safari Press® is registered with the U.S. Patent and Trademark Office and in other countries.

Martínez de Hoz, José A.

First edition

Safari Press Inc.

2005, Long Beach, California

ISBN 1-57157-315-1

Library of Congress Catalog Card Number: 2004094423

10 9 8 7 6 5 4 3 2 1

Printed in Singapore

Readers wishing to receive the Safari Press catalog, featuring many fine books on big-game hunting, wingshooting, and sporting firearms, should write to Safari Press Inc., P.O. Box 3095, Long Beach, CA 90803, USA. Tel: (714) 894-9080 or visit our Web site at www.safaripress.com.

I dedicate this book to all the sporthunters of the world who, with their example of ethical and conservationist hunting, are the best reply to the enemies of hunting—all those who do not understand hunting's true and profound values.

Table of Contents

Preface

I have read many books on big-game hunting in Africa and elsewhere, and I take great pleasure in my collection of hunting books: They were acquired one by one, over the years, as my interest in the subject grew in parallel with my hunting activities. Thus I have biographies of the great hunters and stories of their hunts; accounts of both old-timers and contemporary sportsmen; books on the great game animals, their habits and habitat; and histories of hunting and especially of the African safari.

As I read the books by big-game hunters, it was almost always a famous name—either that of a professional or an amateur sportsman—that attracted my interest and admiration. I had never entertained the idea of writing about my own hunts, because, as an average international hunter, I did not consider them of sufficient interest to the reading public. What's more, I did not enjoy writing about myself, or recounting my hunting exploits.

It was true, though, that friends and family always asked me to talk about my hunts or safaris after they were over. One of my good friends became quite insistent over the years and finally convinced me to allow him to record a series of our conversations. That was how the writing of my big-game hunting reminiscences began.

The argument my friend used, the one that won me over, was very simply that most hunting books are not written by ordinary hunters. Also, most such books tell only the success stories, not the failures. He put it to me that it would be entertaining to many average hunters to read the experiences of someone more like themselves—that is, to learn of the difficulties to expect when going on safari and when hunting different animals with different PHs, whose confidence has to be earned anew on each occasion. That would all be especially true when those experiences were put into the broader context of history, geography, nature, and wildlife—and enriched by a host of interesting personalities—from the Arctic to the tropics and from the plains to the high mountains. Thus this book came into being.

Acknowledgments

My first acknowledgment must go to Edgar (Ed) Howard, without whose friendly insistence in pushing forward his idea and inquisitive and intelligent recording of our conversations these chapters would never have been born.

I have immeasurable appreciation for my wife's patience in putting up with my hunting absences and, in her words, with the "invasion" of my trophies into our city apartment.

I wish to thank all my hunting friends, including the professional hunters and outfitters, who helped me hunt and from whom I have learned so much.

My admiration goes out to all my friends of the Safari Club International, members and staff, for their untiring efforts to promote the principles of ethical hunting and to teach the fundamental connection between conservation and sport hunting.

Last but not least, I wish to record my warm appreciation for the patience and efficiency of Silvana Terenzano and Romina Esteves in the editing and correcting of the transcripts of the recordings.

Chapter 1

Introduction

A Father's Advice

I began big-game hunting fairly late in my life—that is, in my late forties. Previously I had been an enthusiastic feather- or wingshooter. My father was my teacher. He used to take me out Saturdays or Sundays on our country estate. He had the good, old British training, and for one year he made me walk along at his side, with the shotgun open and without firing a shot. The idea was that I learn to hold the weapon properly, never letting it get in the way or pointing it at something I shouldn't, and that I learn how to cross fences with a gun in my hand. The shotgun I carried was always unloaded. I afterward strove to instill the same principles in my own sons, and I found it very effective.

I still keep a copy of a poem that my father had me memorize. Though written at the beginning of the twentieth century, it is still pertinent today.

A Father's Advice

If a sportsman true you'd be, listen carefully to me.
Never, never let your gun pointed be at any one
That it may unloaded be, matters not the least to me.
When a hedge or fence you cross, though of time it cause a loss
From your gun the cartridge take, for the greater safety sake.
If 'twixt you and neighbouring gun, bird may fly or beast may run,
Let this maxim e'er be thine: "Follow not across the line."

A Sporting Life

Stops and beaters, oft unseen, lurk behind some leafy screen
Calm and steady always be, "Never shoot where you can't see."
Keep your place and silent be; Game can hear and game can see.
Don't be greedy, better spared is a pheasant, than one shared.
You may kill, or you may miss, but at all times think of this:
"All the pheasants ever bred won't repay for one man's dead."*

Mark Beaufoy, Member of Parliament, 1909

Learning to Shoot Young

My education began when I was quite young—perhaps ten or a little older. What we had on the country estate were partridge, duck, and hares, nothing much more. I have always thought, and I've confirmed it later in life when big-game hunting, that the person who has begun by using a shotgun and has learned to wingshoot handles a rifle much more easily than someone who has never done so.

Many times one has to shoot with a rifle and telescopic sight at a running animal. That's when experience in wingshooting shines. One must shoot at a flying bird or a running animal with both eyes open, but people who first learn with a rifle generally close their left eye and look down the barrel with their right. I can immediately tell by the way someone holds his rifle if he's been a wingshooter or if he learned to hunt only with a rifle.

Initiation of Hunting with a Rifle

To become a big-game hunter, like many other things in life, one must have a friend, often someone older, to pave the way. It's the sort of thing that one seldom approaches alone, and so it was with me. In my late forties I had a friend, Pedro (Pilicho) Remy Solá, who lived in Salta, a northwestern province of Argentina, and he invited me to hunt guanaco, an animal of the llama family that lives high in

**Mark Beaufoy wrote this poem for his son, Henry, on his thirteenth birthday.*

the Andes. The same region also offers a mountain deer that is very difficult to hunt.

My two eldest sons, who were at the time fifteen and twelve years old, were enthusiastic about coming with me. I didn't have a rifle with a telescopic sight, but my friend told me that he would lend me one. I wanted my boys to have fun, too, and I remembered that my father had given me a very old rifle, one from his days at Eton College in England. It was chambered for the .22 H.P. Savage, considered to be very fast in its day. I still had the gun, and I had a scope mounted on it for use by my eldest son. I borrowed another rifle for my younger son, who could hardly carry it, and off we went. In Salta my friend lent me one of his rifles, a .243 Anschutz, a beautiful little rifle. Thus my sons and I shared the experience of first firing a rifle and looking through a telescopic sight.

My sons José and Marcos loved to hunt, and now they, Pilicho, and I were going up to 13,500 feet in the Andes. My boys and I had never ridden, climbed, or hunted at such an elevation. Normally when up so high one has a problem breathing, and it usually takes a few days to adapt. But in some parts of the Andes because of pressure and other atmospheric conditions, there is in addition the danger of a condition called *puna*. *Puna* is more than just a lack of oxygen. It causes a tremendous headache, a terrible weight on the chest, and a feeling that one is going to die.

Undeterred, we drove to the foothills and mounted mules to begin our ascent. Halfway up we ran into bad weather and had to spend the night in our sleeping bags in the little hut of a gaucho whom Pilicho knew. Next morning a young girl, half Indian, half Creole, came down from the mountains and told us that once through the thick layer of clouds that created a sort of ceiling above us, we would find the weather up there beautiful and sunny. So we saddled up and jumped onto our mules and made the ascent through the clouds. Once above them, we found ourselves surrounded by snowcapped mountains and the most exhilarating view imaginable. It was like being in heaven.

We were above tree line, which is generally about 93,000 feet, and we continued climbing to about 13,500 feet. The terrain was barren and rocky. We had been warned that, when we arrived, we should move slowly, avoid exerting ourselves, and spend the first night quietly, so as to acclimatize ourselves a bit and prevent the *puna*. But once we got to the top, and to a convenient place to tent, it was still daylight, and our gaucho guide immediately found a herd of guanaco nearby. Naturally, we jumped off our mules and begin running up the mountainside to get at them.

A Guanaco Hunt

We took our first shots, which were successful, and brought down our guanacos. The boys and I had wonderful fun. We all felt very proud of ourselves, especially because this was the first time we had shot at an animal with a scoped rifle, and at one point they had been running. But when we descended to the tent that had been erected for us and the evening drew on, I began getting the most horrible headache. It was *puna*, and I'd only myself to blame. The same sort of thing has been known to happen to tourists to Cuzco in Peru, or La Paz in Bolivia.

Puna

I didn't sleep a wink that night, nor could I lie down. All I could manage was to sit up with that terrible headache. I felt that I wanted my head cut off, and the weight on my chest was terrible, but as the hours went by my body gradually adapted. By the next morning, after a most horrible night, I was much better. As to the young boys, they were fine. Nothing ever happens to a twelve- or a fifteen-year-old boy, but I at the time was in my late forties, although in good shape.

In any case, next day we waited until about 10:00 or 11:00 A.M. to head out. We got onto our mules and before long came to a depression in the earth, something like a big sandpit.

I asked our gaucho guide, who was half Indian, half Creole, what it was. He told me that this was where the guanacos roll in the sand. Like any animal, a dog or a horse, he said, they will roll. "And you," he said, looking at me, "if you want to get over your *puna*, you must go and roll in the place where the guanaco rolls. It is the tradition."

Rolling in a Guanaco Sand Pit

That sounded like fun, and of course I didn't want to violate his native beliefs. So I got off my mule, lay down in the sand pit, and began to roll. I didn't notice that Pilicho was ready to play a dirty trick on me. He had his video camera out and took a wonderful sequence of me rolling in the sand like a wild guanaco, as well as a few still photos. Everyone had a good laugh after that. But trick or no, by midday my *puna* was gone.

The guanaco can be a fairly close shot, if one can approach from behind a rock, from about fifty to one hundred yards. It can be a running shot, heart or lung. Or it can be a long shot,

Hunting guanaco above the clouds in the Andean mountains. From left to right: my son Marcos, myself, and Pilicho Remy Solá on our mules above 13,000 feet. Salta Province, Argentina.

if they see the hunter and there's no cover. The most difficult, especially for beginners, is the running shot.

These animals have wonderful wool. All sorts of things are made with it, such as ponchos, jerseys, sweaters, sheepskins, and various other handicrafts. They're really not a trophy animal, though, but rather something for a beginner to have fun with: They have no horns or anything measurable; they're just good practice for beginners. And that was why Pilicho had invited us out.

Sleeping out on the Hillside

We remained out hunting too late on that second day, and our guide got lost in the dark and fog during the ride down the steep mountain path. We could not continue on in the black of night—even the mules refused to go on—and so we dismounted and slept on the hillside. The ground was too steep for a tent, and so we just huddled together, pulling the tent canvas over us like a blanket. All night I kept waking up below the rest; somehow I couldn't help sliding in my sleep.

The Mountain Deer; Sleeping in a Mountain Cave

Pilicho, I learned, had important plans for me with mountain deer, which are a fine trophy animal; they too are found high in the mountains. Locally these deer are called *venado* (the Spanish word for *deer*). They have short and branching, thin horns, and are on the whole rather small animals. In height I would say that they're smaller than an axis deer—rather like a small- to medium-size antelope, running to about thirty inches at the shoulder. Before long, we again went up into the mountains with our mules.

Again there were the most wonderful sights to feast our eyes on, but no matter how much we rode we couldn't find those little deer. And that night we slept in a cave, which was a very large one in the midst of the mountains. We laid our sleeping bags in the deepest recess of the cave, which was the

My son José with the guanaco he took while hunting in the Andean mountains at an altitude of over 13,000 feet. This was the first game animal he ever shot. Salta Province, Argentina.

warmest spot, and we went to sleep. The next morning there was water running over the front of the cave, forming a pinnacle of ice. Negotiating it was quite an adventure for people doing such a thing for the first time.

The following day we came to a place where our guide met a young friend who told him that he knew the whereabouts of a small herd of these deer, down in the valley. The friend said that he had seen them there, and that we should post ourselves at the entrance to it; he would go to the other side and push them toward us.

The Lessons of Hunting

Here we learned a hard lesson: This young boy had a .22 caliber rifle with which he would take small animals. Off he went with his rifle, and we waited there for about five hours. Midday passed, then evening. Finally he came back, very pleased with himself.

"I have wonderful news for you," he said. "I found the deer and I have shot them all for you. Now you can go back to Buenos Aires, and take the meat and the skins. I've done it all for you! You can return with all your trophies."

That, of course, was not exactly what we'd had in mind. But this young boy didn't know. He thought he'd done us a wonderful service.

The Guanaco and the Venado

The guanaco and the *venado* are both species indigenous to Argentina. The guanaco is related to the llama of Peru, as well as to the alpaca and the vicuna—all mountain creatures with lovely, fine wool from which the local population make wonderful ponchos. Nowadays the vicuna are protected, but the guanaco are more numerous and range to lower altitudes. In Patagonia there are many of them, and they compete for grass with the sheep.

The problem is that one guanaco will eat more than two sheep. And after it eats up all that grass, it is really good for nothing, unless it is hunted for its wool or meat. In some provinces they are considered vermin; in others they are protected. By and large, the owners of the land, of the *estancias*, hate them. It's a very odd situation, though, that varies from province to province. In places like Sierra de la Ventana, in the province of Buenos Aires, there are still guanacos there, and one can see them on the skyline while riding or walking in the foothills. They're always up on top, against the skyline like sentries, and it is a wonderful sight seeing the herd silhouetted against the sky.

They are found in many parts of Argentina, except the north. They seem to do well in areas with tough grass and infertile soil. They can live on the very tough grass. But if they find that the grass in the hills is not palatable enough, they will come down and try to eat the sheep's grass. That's when the problems begin.

As to the *venado*, it is the smallest deer in the Andean region, except for the very scarce and minute pudu.

Myself with sons Marcos and José after spending the night in a mountain hut, just before saddling up our mules to continue our ascent for our guanaco hunt. Salta Province, Argentina.

The males have very small spiked horns. These *venado* also at one time had a plains variety, called *venado de las pampas.* They were all over the pampas region and were very abundant, something like the North American whitetail. The problem was that when the country was settled they were hunted both by the Indians and by the settlers—the gauchos—who hunted them for their meat and their skins and in the end virtually wiped them out. Today there are a few reserves in different parts of the country where they are kept as a protected species for breeding purposes.

Chapter 2

A Step toward Africa

The next step in my hunting career was really a very audacious one, because it led me straight to Africa, which my limited experience didn't really justify.

The Blackbuck, or Indian Antelope

Nevertheless, my boys and I were invited by friends and relatives to hunt blackbuck, a species introduced from India. That's why it is also known as the Indian black antelope. It still exists today in India, and it is a true plains game animal. They also can be hunted in game ranches in the United States, but in Argentina they are free-ranging in the pampas.

Blackbuck were introduced early in the twentieth century. They are generally found in open fields, not mountains, and, of course, they have wonderful eyesight. Hunting them means a two- or three-hundred-yard shot, because there is normally no cover to use in approaching them; they will see the hunter from afar and run off, jumping like springbok. They are a wonderful sight to see in any plains area. They are still abundant in Argentina, where they constitute one of the most sporting animals found in that country.

In Spanish, these animals are called *antílope negro*, or *antílope de la India*. They have two spiral, straight horns that twist upward like corkscrews. The more twists, the better the trophy. In a straight line the horns are about 19–23 inches high, although they come to more than 30 inches if they are measured around the corkscrew rings. The blackbuck is no more than 14 inches deep from the top of the shoulder to the elbow—that is, a girth of 14 inches and a shoulder height of 25 inches. Their weight is under 110 pounds, no more. They are definitely small animals for a 300-yard shot.

Blackbuck were introduced by Argentine sportsmen, who also introduced the red and axis deer. At the turn of the nineteenth century, there were many Argentine sportsmen who wanted to hunt according to British or German tradition, and this seemed like the answer. Once the blackbuck were introduced, they thrived. They have a high fertility rate, so they multiply enormously—so much so that in our day many *estancias,* or ranches, find them a problem; blackbuck become too numerous by feeding on the special oats or grasses sown to fatten steers. Oftentimes the owners of the *estancias* will call in packing houses to cull them, and then the packing houses will sell the meat to the public. Blackbuck are now found all over the pampas region, and recent sport hunting laws have enabled landowners to cull their population by opening their properties to hunting; the trophy fee, incidentally, produces useful extra revenue.

A jumping herd of blackbuck at full gallop. The females and young males are fawn in color, and the males turn black as they mature. Buenos Aires Province, Argentina.

A mature male blackbuck, as seen above, is a very sporting free-range trophy and generally requires a long shot in open, grassy plains. Buenos Aires Province, Argentina.

General Thoughts about Sport Hunting

Organized hunting does not drive a species to extinction if properly managed. On the contrary, populations of wild animals thrive when they are hunted in this way. The United States offers a very good example. Statistics that have been widely publicized, especially by the Safari Club International, show that at the beginning of the twentieth century there were about 500,000 white-tailed deer in the United States. Nowadays, after the institution of organized hunting, there are more than 30 million. And whitetails are the most hunted species in the United States.

Why has their population grown so? The answer: The system of organized hunting takes into consideration the population census of the animals, and it authorizes quotas by which the wildlife authority regulates the hunt. Furthermore, the money paid by sportsmen to hunt the animals works its way back into the system and stimulates people to take care of them—because to do so is profitable. Thus instead of simply being killed, the animals are cultivated because they have an economic value; it is known what they are worth to the hunter who comes looking for a trophy. I have read that in some places in the United States the whitetails are so numerous that they have reached the outskirts of cities, where they cause a traffic hazard.

The Mistake of Banning Hunting

Those people who wish to forbid hunting fail to understand that when the sport hunter or the professional hunter is locked out, the only hunter who will take the game will be the poacher, who hunts for meat and hides and will happily drive a species to extinction. The secret is that the animal must have an economic value, and its numbers must be regulated, if it is to thrive in today's world. Once the animal has an economic value placed on it because hunters will pay for the privilege of pursuing their sport, it will be protected by both the local population and the hunters themselves. Local people will become guides, or offer lodging or other hunting-related goods and services. A legal hunt produces economic activity of many kinds.

A good example is Brazil. Jaguar hunting in Brazil used to be popular—there are lots of jaguars there. A number of years ago, however, jaguar and most other hunting was forbidden in Brazil. Today all that is permitted is bird hunting in the state of Rio Grande do Sul. The result? Nowadays there are more jaguars shot illegally than in the past were hunted legally. If the hunt had been kept legal, it would have produced valuable revenue for the region and effectively protected the jaguar.

Chapter 3

Off to Africa

After hunting the northwestern province of Salta, my two sons and I continued our education for about a year, hunting blackbuck in the pampas and red deer in our southern mountain and lake region. It was very sporty and good training.

By this time I had traveled to the United States and bought two rifles with the advice of a good friend who was a big-game hunter and had been going to Africa for more than ten years running. When he saw that I too had become interested in big game, he began to give me advice, culminating with the necessary tips as to rifles, scopes, and the rest.

My friend was Arturo Acevedo, the son of the founder and chairman of Acindar Steel Corporation; he was the head of its production division. He sent me to a gun shop in New York, one that no longer exists, called Zirmo. It was downtown, on Warren Street near Wall Street, and I became a client for quite a few years. I also made purchases from Continental Arms on Fifth Avenue. Following his advice, I bought two rifles: One was of medium caliber, a .308. When he had in mind inviting me to join him in Africa, he had me purchase a .375 as well.

Those were my first rifles. They were both Belgian, the .375 a Belgian Browning and the .308 a Belgian F.N., which is their Fabrique Nationale; I later had the F.N. recalibered to a .300 Winchester Magnum. Little by little, on subsequent trips to the States or to Europe, I improved upon my equipment, acquiring new rifles as circumstances or necessity demanded.

PH Peter Behr and Glen Cottar pretending to eat his birthday cake made with elephant dung during my first African safari. Even though evening temperatures were chilly, the companionship was very warm. Kenya.

An Invitation to Hunt in Africa

When Arturo Acevedo Sr. died, I was invited in 1968 by the board of directors to become chairman of Acindar. Near the end of 1975, Arturo Jr. invited my elder son and me to join him in Africa for his annual hunt. Of course, I jumped at the chance.

Arturo used to hunt with a very well known professional hunter by the name of Glen Cottar, one of the top professionals in Africa. I would be taking with me my eldest son, José, who was eighteen at the time. How I wished my father had taken me to Africa when I was eighteen! In early 1976 we left for a forty-day safari to Kenya; nowadays if one has fifteen days one can be considered lucky.

Hunting in Kenya

Kenya was a paradise for big-game hunting. I was very fortunate to see it and to be able to hunt, because, as it turned out, that was the last year in which Kenya was open to hunting.

The year before they had received a visit from Prince Bernard of Holland, who was head of the WWF, the World Wildlife Fund, a very important conservation group of which I am a member—although I recognize that sometimes they can be a bit theoretical in their approach. Prince Bernard said that elephants should be protected, and it's an ongoing dispute to this day. Nevertheless, the Kenyan government forbade elephant hunting, and the year I was there, 1976, was the first year in which the prohibition came into effect. One could hunt everything else, but not elephant. The next year, all hunting was banned.

The Fate of Elephants of Kenya

Before sport hunting had been closed for elephant, each year there had been three hundred licenses issued in Kenya to sport hunters to hunt three hundred elephants. In the following four years, thirty thousand elephants were shot . . . shot, not hunted. Even the wife of Jomo Kenyatta, the famous hero of the Mau Mau rebellion and the first president of Kenya, wanted to partake of the ivory trade with Hong Kong and other Far Eastern ports. This debacle marked the end of elephant with good ivory in Kenya. The ecologists and protectionists who had applauded the "wonderful" way in which Kenya had protected its wildlife were proved wrong, but the realization came too late.

Nairobi

Nairobi was an attractive city. I've always liked Nairobi. In those days one could still feel the lingering British colonial traditions, which President Kenyatta had maintained: the discipline in the main streets, the way that life went on, the business hustle, the shops, and the merchants, all of whom, of course, were Hindus. In that way it was quite typical of many African countries. There were still traditional hotels that went right back to the beginnings of the safari industry.

The first hotel in Nairobi was the Norfolk Hotel, which at that time was already half abandoned and on the outskirts of the city. The hotel where we were staying was the New Stanley, or Thorntree Hotel—it had a big thorntree, with thorns longer than one's finger, in the middle of a sort of patio where one had cocktails. The Thorntree patio and the bar at the hotel were great meeting places both for professional hunters looking for their clients and for those professional hunters who were looking for new clients; as a result, there was a lot of atmosphere. It made one remember all the stories about the days of the old safaris.

Life in Nairobi was very pleasant. We went to see Glen Cottar's house, on the outskirts of town, which was very nice and had large grounds with beautiful bougainvillea plants—or Santa Rita, as we call them in the Argentine. His wife, Pat, took us to see where they bloom and to visit a professional plant grower, who had the most beautiful variety of every color. In addition, all the streets and the park in Nairobi were covered with bougainvillea bushes and trees. I bought quite a few of these bougainvillea branches of different colors with the purpose of replanting them, hoping that they would thrive back home, where only a single color grows. What happened was incredible. I had them planted, and great care was taken of them to protect them from frosts. But as they grew they lost their original color and turned into the single color that can be seen in Argentina, a mauvish red. Perhaps it's something in the soil.

The outskirts of Nairobi were beautiful, especially the Ngong Hills (pronounced *in-gong*), where Glen Cottar's place was located. The Ngong Hills are known to many who otherwise might never have heard of them because of Karen Blixen—that is, Isak Dinesen. Her book (and later the film) *Out of Africa* describes her farm there. That is where Denys Finch-Hatton, the famous professional hunter she loved, was buried when he lost his life in an airplane crash.

When Jomo Kenyatta died, they erected an immense statue of him in the public park in Nairobi. As for the other national hero of the Mau Mau rebellion, Kimathi, there was a street named for him. But at the same time there was a statue in remembrance of the Kenyan soldiers that had died in both of the world wars fighting with the British Army. Thus the city was a blend of what was left of British influence plus the new elements that were on the way in. Later they built the big Nairobi convention center, where many international conventions have been held.

Hunting in Kenya

We had a wonderful time hunting in Kenya. The hunting there was organized very efficiently. President Kenyatta had been very intelligent and had respected many of the old-time British traditions that had ruled hunting for many years since its inception in East Africa.

For example, there was the golden rule of hunting, applicable really to any sort of hunting, which states that the animal and the hunter should each have a 50–50 chance. That is to say, the animal should have the chance of escaping or of charging the hunter, and the hunter a 50 percent chance of taking the animal. It's called "fair hunt," meaning that nothing should be done that is unethical. There is an ethical basis to sport hunting.

British traditions, such as not shooting from a vehicle, were very wise. When they have photographic safaris nowadays in the national parks, the animals don't seem to mind having a lot of people about—as long as they stay in their vehicles. The smell of the combustion engine masks the human scent to which wild animals react first by flight and second by attacking.

That is why, when they visit these parks, people are told never to leave the vehicle. If they do, in the middle of a park where there are dangerous animals, something unexpected might happen. There was a famous film called *Mondo Cane*, which means "a dog's world." It highlighted some of these catastrophes.

One of them occurred in Kenya, when a photographic safari was going through a park where there was a group of lions nearby. A tourist, not heeding the instructions, got down from the vehicle to take photos. But he went too far. A man in the vehicle had a video camera, and he recorded how the sightseer was mauled, killed, and eaten by the lions in front of his wife and children. That tragedy demonstrates just how unsporting it is to shoot from a vehicle. The old rule was that you had to be at least a thousand yards from the vehicle to shoot.

After the death of Jomo Kenyatta, British traditions faded. Nowadays Kenya has photographic safaris, which are lovely, but there is no hunting at all.

Life in an African Hunting Camp

A few words on hunting camps in Africa may be of interest. Modern camps are different from those of twenty or twenty-five years ago. My first hunt in Kenya, back in 1976, was the nicest hunt one can imagine. How were the facilities? Before dawn, in the dark, there was a knock on the tent and in came the waiter saying in Swahili, "*Jambo, chai?*"—that is, "Hello, tea?" According to English tradition, tea gives one the strength to get up. Washing was accomplished in a basin of water outside the tent and shaving was managed with a little mirror on a tent pole.

The bathroom was a small tent with a hole dug in the floor over which stood a small stool with no middle, just the round edge on which to sit. Afterward ashes were put onto whatever happened to be in the hole. The first job of the apprentice PH (professional hunter) was to dig the hole.

On one of his previous safaris, Arturo Acevedo went to the toilet tent one evening and a few seconds later there was a loud yell. His son rushed into the toilet tent with a shotgun and a flashlight and saw his father sitting on the stool. Rising up out of the hole was a black mamba, one of the most venomous snakes in Africa. Arturo's son immediately shot the mamba but in doing so also shot a couple of legs off the stool. Arturo ended up falling with his backside in the hole, on top of the black mamba, which fortunately was dead. At the time, he said, the incident was considered quite amusing.

The Shower Tent

If one wanted a shower after a day's hunting, there was another tent that offered a canvas bag with a showerhead at the end of it. A loud yell would bring someone with shower water. Warm water was not really necessary, except on cold nights, because, being out in the sun all day, the water was half warm anyway. I have very good memories of those showers. When you pulled on a bit of rope, the bag tilted and the water came down. It lasted for only a few minutes, so you really had to soap yourself quickly.

A Whiskey around the Campfire

And then came one of the nicest parts of the day—that is, sitting around the campfire with a glass of whiskey in one's hand. And then the campfire conversation began. Everybody told a story, either the largest lie they could think of or a real story. One sat there for about half an hour and then went to dinner. Prince Otto von Bismarck, the famous German statesman, once said that the largest amount of lies are told when a politician is campaigning for office, a general is recounting his battle achievements, or a hunter is relating his hunts.

Food and Water

For dinner there was a mess tent, the kind the army used. And the cooks generally weren't very good. The best thing to eat was the game—antelope, impala, gazelle, or whatever one had had the luck to bring into camp. Buffalo meat is tough, and only the tongue is generally fit to eat, although oxtail soup is very good. The natives, of course, ate all the meat they could get, even buffalo. Lion meat is tough and stringy. In the absence of fresh meat, one had only canned or dried foods.

Hyenas at Night

One of the first experiences one has with animals in Africa is often with the hyena. On the first night, the staff would advise the clients to zip up the tent flap securely; if not, a hyena might come in and run off with a safari boot or something else chewable. Soon the concert of hyena cackling would begin—the howling and the rest of the noises. Sometimes the hyena would come right up to the tent and scratch the sides with their paws, trying to get in. One soon got used to it, though; it was all part of the fun.

Modern Comfort

Things are very different today. There are basically two sorts of camps. Many have what are called rondavels, which are permanent little huts built of cane or sticks and covered with dry mud with a thatched roof. Inside, one sleeps in a real bed, not on a cot. Other camps, like the one I was in recently in Botswana in the Okavango, have permanent tents. They, too, are far more comfortable than in the old days. In addition, camps today are much more organized and civilized than when I first visited Africa.

Camps today can be permanent or movable. The one in the Okavango Delta was more or less fixed. The tents there were not on dirt but on cement platforms. And there were good beds. There was even a flush toilet, just like at home, right inside the tent. There was a shower inside the tent, too. Just turn the tap, and there's the water. It's all very modern and comfortable, but the truth is that roughing it was really much more fun. I suppose that these changes have been brought about by the great affluence of so many hunters. Americans have probably accounted for a lot of the change; they have wanted the comfort and could pay for it, so outfitters adapted to their wishes.

Kenya was a hunting paradise then, not only because of its natural beauty and wildlife but also because of its organization. Professional hunters were given concessions that lasted for so

Here I am standing in front of my tent, which I shared with my son José, at our first camp in the Loita Hills. Masai Mara, Kenya.

many years that they could make serious improvements, such as good access roads to the blocks of land they had been given. It was really a very clever and sensible way of doing things.

To return to my first African hunt, I went, as I have said, with Arturo Acevedo, one of Arturo's sons, and my son José. Glen Cottar was a top professional hunter who always took Arturo out on safari, and a young associate hunter by the name of Peter Behr took care of us. He was very good, although quite young.

Peter had been born in the Seychelles Islands and then had lived in Kenya. He was my first professional hunter. After the independence of African nations, the term "white hunter" could no longer be used, and organizations like Cottar's were obliged to engage at least one black hunter. Now they were all called "professional hunters."

Relations between Professional Hunters and Clients

Good professional hunters have to be clever. They take on clients from all over the world, and they don't know if they are good hunters or not—if they can shoot straight, if they are disciplined, or if they have the necessary guts. Generally, they will test the client, which is good for both parties: The PH gets to know the caliber of his client, and the client has the opportunity to win the confidence of the PH.

The first thing my son and I were called upon to do was to hunt a Tommy—that is, a Thomson gazelle, the smallest gazelle in Kenya. It is a very beautiful little animal, and very agile. We were asked to shoot one with my .375, which is a big caliber the bullet from which begins to drop substantially at 150 yards. So a 250- or 300-yard shot at a Tommy is difficult, especially for a beginner.

Well, we passed that first exam, and we went on to hunt a Grant gazelle, which is a little larger but also very beautiful. Gradually we worked our way up the ladder, moving on to wildebeest, a big, ugly creature, and then to other nondangerous game animals.

There was the hartebeest, or *kongoni*, and the zebra, which is not easy to hunt because it is alert and skittish. Then there are other antelopes and gazelles, the beautiful jumping impalas, the waterbuck, and small animals like the warthog, which with their long tusks could be called the wild boar of Africa. They are a difficult shot because they are very quick. Those were all species found in the Masai Mara area, where we were hunting in the Loita Hills. Toward the end of the safari we moved to Lake Magadi especially for fringe-eared oryx. The wonderful thing for a beginner in this part of Kenya was that almost every day one went out to hunt a different animal. That's quite another thing from safaris in which weeks might be spent hunting only elephant, or searching for a very special trophy such as mountain nyala.

We were working our way up to buffalo, leopard, and lion, for which we had licenses. We could take two buffalo, which I consider one of the most sporting and also most dangerous animals to hunt. I would say that the three most dangerous animals are first the elephant, second the buffalo (Cape buffalo or dwarf forest buffalo), and third the grizzly bear or the brown bear of the north (be it Alaska, Europe, or Russia).

Harmonizing the Personalities of the PH and His Client

As to the relationship between the PH and his client, drawing from my own experience I would say that the harmonizing of personalities is very important. On one of my later safaris in Africa I went to Zimbabwe with two friends, and the outfitting company provided three very good professional hunters, each of them, as might have been expected, quite different. One of my friends, Héctor Pefaur, had hunted in Africa several times, twice with me in Ethiopia for elephant and mountain nyala. He was an easygoing person, and although he didn't speak a word of English he managed to make himself understood and got on well with his PH.

My other friend's case was different. He was an excellent shot and an experienced hunter from Argentina, where he hunted mainly red stag. As he knew the areas in which he hunted, he was accompanied there only by a helper, not by a guide or much less by a PH. This was to be his first safari in Africa, and although the basic principles of hunting are the same the world over, when the hunter is out in unknown territory he needs a PH. That is especially true if, as in this case, he wishes to take dangerous animals such as buffalo, leopard, and lion.

I have learned in Africa that, in addition to earning the confidence of the PH, one must obey his instructions: He is responsible for one's life and for the success of the hunt. In a

Here we are standing around the border demarcation between Tanzania and Kenya. From right to left: my son José, young Rafael Acevedo, Glen Cottar, and Arturo Acevedo. We hunted in the Toyota that can be seen in the background. Kenya.

word, he is the captain of the ship. Obviously, both client and PH must try to adapt their personalities to each other in order to avoid problems. In this case my friend, being used to hunting alone and to being his own master, at first had some difficulty in adjusting to the situation, all the more so because at home he worked as a public prosecutor in the judiciary and was used to exercising authority and giving orders. In short, he had a rather strong personality.

On the other hand, his PH was a young Zimbabwean of Boer origin who, like most of his ancestors, had an inflexible and rather harsh character. Perhaps he stretched his responsibilities too far, though, in insisting that his client stay in the vehicle when he himself got down to glass a group of animals. Of course his doing so deprived the client of a large part of the fun of the hunt. This situation, together with a few other irritations of a similar nature, gradually built up into a serious disagreement. After a few discussions in which the client found himself at a disadvantage for not being fluent in English, on the third day of the safari there was an explosion.

On the evening in question I was the last hunter to return to camp, and Héctor immediately called me into his tent and explained that our friend had decided that he would not continue to be treated like a child by a "young upstart PH" and would therefore end his safari and return home. That, of course, we could not accept; it would also ruin our own hunt. Héctor therefore begged me to use all of my diplomatic abilities to sort things out with the PH in English; he suspected that there was some language misunderstanding that was making matters worse than they had to be.

I found the PH at the campfire and tried to get him to understand my friend's point of view. I emphasized that although this was his first safari in Africa he was not a beginner but an accomplished and experienced hunter and should be treated as such. I told him that if he could be more flexible, I would also tell my friend that he should understand that the PH is the captain of the ship and that his reasonable instructions should be followed. I finally got them both to agree and to shake hands. At the campfire that night we toasted a successful safari.

Fly Camps and Dangerous Ants

One of the delights of tenting in Africa is that one must be very careful not to put the tent on top of an anthill. There are two sorts of ants in Africa—at least two that are normally found. The black soldier ants, the big ones, are sometimes found marching like the *marabunta*, which can eat a whole area clean and look like a massive army column on the move. The natives use the strong grip of the ants' jaws to suture wounds.

But the most dangerous ants are the red ants, which are much smaller; if you find them crawling up your body the only thing to do is to undress quickly and brush them off. There have been cases in which red ants have crawled into the nose or ears of a baby and from there into the brain—and that child is dead. Red ants are quite as dangerous, in their way, as a big animal.

In the book *Inside Safari Hunting* by Dennis Holman, a famous PH by the name of Eric Rundgren recalls that he once took out on safari a rather competitive married couple. The wife was a beautiful woman and a very good shot, better than her husband. Eric and she were hunting a lion, and they entered a donga, a clump of bushes of sorts. This one was about a hundred yards long and half as wide. The husband had remained behind.

Suddenly there were red ants climbing up them, inside their clothes. So Eric told the woman to strip, to get her clothes off as quickly as possible. It's the only thing you can do to save yourself from the ants, he explained. She did, and just then her husband arrived on the scene.

That was the end of the hunt. It was also the end of the safari, and maybe the marriage. I don't know.

The Origins of the Modern Safari

The safari industry, as such, did not exist before the twentieth century. The word *safari* in Swahili means "trip" or "journey." And the man who made the word popular was

Taking a Thomson gazelle. José Jr. and PH Peter Behr. Kenya.

none other than Teddy Roosevelt. He made his famous safari in 1909, the eleven-month safari for which he declined reelection as president of the United States.

It's an extraordinary story. Roosevelt had been vice president, and when President McKinley was assassinated he became president. Thus he completed McKinley's term and then was elected president on his own merits. When that term ended in 1909 he was up for reelection, but he declined a seemingly easy electoral victory because he wanted to go on safari to Africa. It was his big ambition. Just imagine.

He was, of course, a great outdoorsman. Roosevelt had expanded the National Parks System in the United States, established wildlife refuges, and founded the Boone and Crockett *Records of North American Big Game.* He was an enthusiastic hunter-conservationist who loved the wilderness. He read a lot about hunting, and he corresponded with African hunters such as Frederick Selous and began preparing over the course of two or three years for the safari he had in mind. Then he turned down a second term as president.

Roosevelt's safari lasted eleven months. It was the largest safari ever to leave Nairobi. It was sponsored by Washington's Smithsonian Institution and included a large number of zoologists and botanists to collect and study specimens. Roosevelt was authorized to shoot a male and female of every species for the Smithsonian and the Museum of Natural History in New York. He could do the same for himself as well. Andrew Carnegie contributed handsomely to the financing of the expedition, and T. R. paid his own expenses and those of his twenty-year-old son Kermit by writing a series of articles for *Scribner's* magazine that were published as a book in 1910 under the title *African Game Trails.* The *New York Herald Tribune* declared it the book of the year.

The hunting community was tremendously gratified that this former president of the United States should go on safari. As a result, a group of British sportsmen, hunters, and naturalists got together and presented him with a double rifle, a Holland & Holland .500-450 Nitro Express. Among the donors were Buxton, Lord Averbury, Lord Lonsdale, St. George Littledale, two Rothchilds, the Duke of Bedford, and, of course, Frederick Selous. This famous double rifle came up for auction in New York quite recently when a grandson of Kermit's sold it.

African Game Trails caused a furor all over the hunting world. I have a first edition printing that I was lucky to acquire in London at Rowland Ward's. In it there is a famous photo of T. R. with his son Kermit, sitting on their first buffalo. Kermit later became a very important international hunter in his own right, hunting in Asia and elsewhere. Anyway, it is a very, very interesting book.

It was Teddy Roosevelt's writings that popularized the name "safari." Before, it really wasn't widely known. Although safari means a journey in Swahili, it became known as a hunt organized for clients, for paying clients or invited clients or guest clients or whatever, but not just an explorer or hunter by himself. That's the difference.

He entered through Mombasa, on the coast of Kenya, and went up by the Uganda railway to Nairobi, where he was received enthusiastically. The safari was organized with two or three professional hunters and a host of porters, in the old fashion. He finished at Khartoum, eleven months later.

Chapter 4

The Big Five

When speaking of dangerous animals in Africa, the first that come to mind are the so-called Big Five: elephant, buffalo, lion, leopard, and rhinoceros. However, today it is forbidden to hunt rhinoceros in the wild just about everywhere. The black rhinoceros, which was the most numerous and most aggressive, has been killed to near extinction because its horn is actually hair, not bone. It is formed of pressed hair, and it is

Evening celebration at our fly camp after I took my lion and Arturo Acevedo took his black rhino on the same day. From left to right: my son José, Arturo Acevedo, young Rafael Acevedo, PH Peter Behr, Glen Cottar, and myself. Kenya.

believed by many to have aphrodisiac properties. Thus there was a big demand in the East for it, and now the black rhino is almost gone.

In South Africa, game ranches are considering breeding them as they did with the white rhino. As to the differences between the two, apart from color, the black rhino is a browser, eating the leaves of trees, and it is the more aggressive of the two species. The white rhino is bigger and has a wide mouth. Its name comes from the Dutch word meaning "wide." It is a grazer, eating grass.

In recent years South African game ranches have rebuilt the white rhino population. Nowadays white rhinos can be hunted in South Africa, but to do so is pricey—around $30,000. Of course these animals have been bred in game ranches and obviously are not completely wild, although some of the ranches can provide a sporting hunt.

Shaking hands with PH Peter Behr after taking my 46-inch Cape buffalo. It was a strenuous hunt. Kenya.

Glen Cottar and Arturo Acevedo with the horns of Arturo's black rhino back at our fly camp. Kenya.

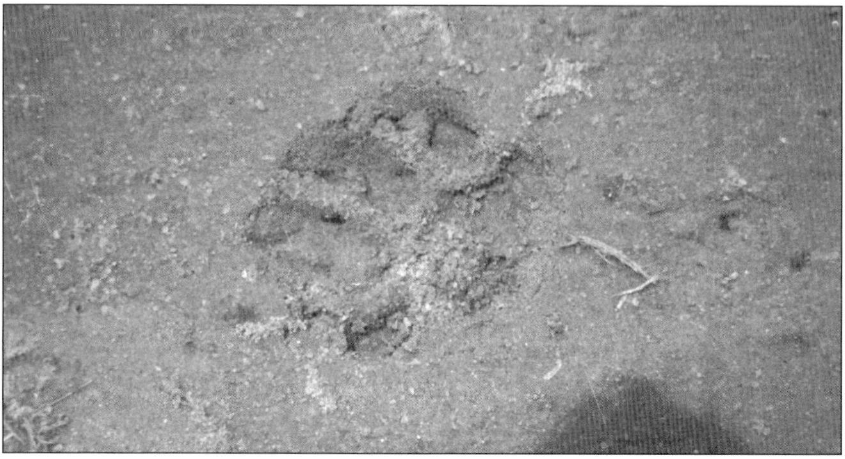

This footprint in a sand river is of the lion that we were following and that, subsequently, I shot. Kenya.

Really, one should talk of the Big Four, because the rhino cannot be hunted in the wilderness any more. Nowadays they are beginning to dart rhinos, which, in addition to conservation considerations, is really more dangerous and exciting. The rifles that fire the darts have a very short range—normally not more than fifty yards.

Incidentally, in the year that we went to Kenya, 1976, my friend Arturo took a very good black rhino. Of course he kept the horn as a trophy—not for use as an aphrodisiac.

Our Buffalo Hunt

To return to our safari, after we passed the test with gazelles and antelopes, Peter Behr, our PH, decided that we could go on to hunt dangerous animals. One early morning, glassing a hill near our camp, we saw a group of five bachelor buffaloes at the top, one of which was especially good. It was about a 500-foot climb up, and once we got there they had disappeared. They had obviously heard us approaching. So we followed their tracks, up and down hills, through thick brush and thorn trees. At midday we caught up with them. They were grazing in a valley, and we were above them on a hill. So as to approach quietly, only Peter and I went down, taking off everything that might make a noise in the brush. In spite of all our care, however, as soon as we got near the buffaloes they stampeded through the valley, felling everything in their path. After the five-hour walk back to camp, circling the foothills, we decided to try again the next day. It took us three tough days before I was able to get a shot at that buffalo; it turned out to be a very old bull with horns of over forty-six inches. Over the course of the next two days, my son José was able to take his buff in much the same way. They were both exciting and tiring hunts.

A Buffalo-Hunting Accident

During that first safari in Kenya we met a friend, Billy Louge, who was in the diplomatic corps at the Argentine embassy in Nairobi. He was a very good and avid hunter, especially of buffalo, and he showed us around and gave us some useful tips. At the end of our safari, when we got back to Nairobi and tried to contact him, we were told that he was in the Nairobi Hospital. Of course we went to visit him, and we found him in bed with a bandage on one of his legs.

He had gone out on a short buffalo hunt with Tony Seth-Smith, a well known PH who was a friend of his. They were following buffalo tracks when suddenly out of the long grass a buffalo charged and sent them both flying into the air. They were just able to place quick shots into its neck, but that did not stop it. It knelt over Billy, who was flat on the ground and quite defenseless, and tried to gore him. The buffalo was not successful, though, as the shots in the neck apparently had impaired the mobility of its head. After a while—which must have seemed an eternity—the buffalo got up and walked away, leaving both hunters miraculously unscathed.

"Then why are you in the hospital?" we asked. It seems that in the scuffle on the ground, a piece of burning wood, left by the locals and still glowing, had got into his safari boot. By the time he noticed it, his heel had been badly burned. It seemed a tremendous irony that having escaped by miracle from a buffalo charge, Billy was now in hospital with burns on his foot.

I took this 9-foot, 7-inch lion in a donga with my Browning .375 rifle. From left to right: PH Peter Behr, myself, and tracker Arap Sambu. Kenya.

On Lions and Leopards

Apart from the buffaloes, we had only two additional licenses for dangerous animals. One was for a lion and the other a leopard. I chose the lion, and my son José obviously had to take second choice. But he was a good sport, in addition to being an excellent shot and a very good hunter. He got the leopard.

In those days lion in Kenya were hunted in a very sporting way, which nowadays is practiced only in Botswana. We had to find tracks or spoor and follow them. In most countries today, such as Tanzania or Zimbabwe, lion are baited. However, baiting for lion was forbidden in Kenya at the time. Leopard could be baited, because it is a nocturnal animal. A dead game animal—antelope, gazelle, warthog, zebra, wildebeest, or impala previously shot for the purpose—was used.

In Tanzania, which was like Kenya, it used to be forbidden to bait for lions. Nowadays, however, the professional hunters have become numerous and take on a lot of clients. They want to make money quickly, and of course it takes longer to find a lion by following its tracks than by putting up a bait and hunting it like a leopard. So that's what they do.

The only country where lions can still be hunted by following spoor is Botswana. That tradition lingers because Botswana has sandy soil, in which tracks can be easily followed. So they keep up the tradition and are very proud of it.

Chapter 5

The Hunt for a Lion

The lion area was not in the immediate vicinity of our base camp, and so a "fly camp" was used. All our party came, including Glen Cottar and Arturo, who was out to get a black rhino, for which he had a license.

We were in two groups, each of which had a Toyota Land Cruiser, a tracker, and a skinner—very good men. Our PH was Peter Behr; Glen Cottar was PH for Arturo. On safari a hunter might go 1x1, which means one PH and one client, or 2x1, which is two clients and one PH. That was the case for me and my son, and we took turns hunting, which is the usual procedure on 2x1 hunts.

Incidentally, two brothers who were friends of ours had hunted with Glen a month before we did. So we got all the chitchat from Glen about their hunt. They went 2x1, but with an incredible arrangement: Instead of agreeing to take one animal each or to hunt on alternate days, they arranged to hunt by the hour. If, for example, they were following a lion, just at the moment one of them was about to fire the other might say, "Hey, time's up. It's my shot."

That's the most outrageous plan for a hunt that I have ever heard of. But I guess it was great fun, at least to hear the way Glen Cottar told the story.

The Roar of the Lion

Every night, we heard the lions roar. There is an old saying that a lion hunter gets frightened three times: the first time is when he hears the lion roar; the second time is when he sees its tracks; and the third time is when he sees the lion. On this occasion there were two lions—at least we heard two different roars near our camp. We heard them every night. Of course we went out at first light, looking for their spoor, but we couldn't find them. And this went on, day after day. Although it was a forty-day hunt, we had set a time limit of one week for the lion and one week for the leopard. The lion week was coming to an end, and I was starting to get worried.

Lion Tracks in a Sand River

On the sixth day, the last but one, we suddenly came across very big lion tracks in a sand river. Sand rivers are famous in Africa because in the dry season the rivers dry up, but water flows under the sand. These sand rivers actually have freshwater running under their sand.

These were very fresh tracks. As we crossed the river and ascended a little hill, we spotted a couple of lions, one male and one female. At that time one could be very choosy; things are different now. This particular lion didn't have a black mane. It was a good one, though, and we were wondering whether I should shoot it when another pair showed themselves. The new male had a very nice mane, better than the first. That, we said, is the one.

And then all four lions entered a donga, an ellipse of low brush and small trees in the middle of which were gnarls and the stumps of trees. They went in at one end, and we circled and went in at the other. There were four lions inside, but we didn't know where they were.

A Sleeping Lion

Suddenly, we saw the good lion at the far end. It was lying down, with the lioness standing alongside. We were about a hundred yards away when my PH said, "There it is. Shoot."

I have never shot an animal that is lying down, and I just didn't like the idea. So I said to Peter, "Let's wait for him to get up."

I had just spoken when the female, who must have scented our wind, pawed the male and they both rose quickly and left the donga. The things my PH said to me when that happened may not be reproduced in these pages.

A Good Heart Shot

Although I had let the lion go, and after spending so many days looking for it, I was very fortunate. God was kind to me that day. Having left the donga, the two lions then reentered, a little nearer than before. Now they were only seventy yards off. And there they both stood, the lion very majestic with the female at its side. Arap Sambu, our tracker, couldn't stop himself from whispering aloud *"Piga, Piga!"* (shoot!), and I didn't doubt. I got off a quick shot with my .375, a heart shot, and the lion went down. *"M'zuri Sana,"* (very good) exclaimed Sambu.

The lion has thin skin, and if a shot is well placed in a vital spot the animal will fall immediately. If it is a bad shot that only wounds, the lion will most likely run and hide in the long grass or in the bush. Then you have to go after it, often not knowing exactly where it is. At that point the lion becomes very dangerous. It can charge at a speed of forty-five miles per hour, and it is not easy to stop one with a frontal shot because it doesn't have a flat face like a buffalo.

After the lion was down, the lioness wouldn't leave. The female seemed to think that the lion was sleeping and kept pawing at it. We couldn't go up to the lion to skin it or get photographs, because the female was there. In fact, lionesses are really much more aggressive than males (some people would say that is the case with all females). We finally began throwing stones outside the donga to divert her attention, and she left.

We went up to the lion at last, and after the photo session our skinner, Getet, began his work. We had to stand by with our rifles ready in case the lioness came back.

This was a very good lion. It was 9 feet, 7 inches long, and it made the African edition of *Rowland Ward's Records of Big Game.*

Chapter 6

Deserving a Lion

Another lion story might be of interest here. This one took place during my Kenya safari, but before I had taken my lion. One morning we awoke at our main camp on a day when we were to hunt buffalo. It was February—winter in Kenya—and normally we got up at 6:30 for breakfast and then went off.

At 6:00 A.M.—it had been a rainy night—we were awakened by an incredible row and loud shouting in French and English that went on for about half an hour until it finally subsided. At breakfast we found Glen Cottar and asked him, "Glen, what happened?" He answered, "Oh, that was a French client that

We were hunting fringe-eared oryx when we came upon this herd of giraffe in the Lake Magadi region, where we had gone to hunt. The rocky wall of the escarpment is in the background. Kenya.

François Giscard d'Estaing hunting red stag with me in our southern mountain region during Easter week, April 1979. He was an avid African elephant hunter and president of the lion hunters club in Paris. Neuquén Province, Argentina.

was furious because he has been here for fifteen days and hasn't been able to get his lion." This was the story.

The Club of Lion Hunters

This Frenchman had come out for a fifteen-day lion-only hunt; he was not interested in anything else. It seemed that there was a club in Paris of which you could become a member only if you had shot a lion. Former president of France Valéry Giscard d'Estaing's cousin, François, was its president. This Frenchman was a real snob, someone who wanted to become a member of that prestigious club, and he had come out to Africa to shoot a lion.

Unfortunately for him, that was the worst reason he might have given to Glen Cottar—or to any other PH—for wanting to hunt. It meant that he was no real hunter, and the PHs began by despising him. The worst thing that can happen to a hunter is to have the PH despise him, because the success of the hunt depends on the PH.

Elephants at a water hole in the Matetsi area during my elephant hunt there. Zimbabwe.

So this Frenchman began with very bad marks against him. Inasmuch as they were nearing the area where the PH already had leopard baits up, the PH asked this man if he wanted to sit up for a leopard, and he agreed. So the Frenchman and his PH began to watch a bait that afternoon, but when sundown approached, the light started to fade, the bush noises increased, and the level of excitement started to rise, the Frenchman began to get nervous.

After a time he got so nervous that he gave his rifle to his PH and said, "Look, whatever comes, you shoot it, and we'll say I did." Wrong again. The PH didn't shoot the leopard, and the man was out. But they didn't send him home. They kept him for his whole term of fifteen days, got his money on the daily rate, and never took him anywhere near a lion.

So what we had heard was the end of the hunt. He never saw a lion, never fired a shot, and was furious. He had a heated discussion in French with Glen Cottar, saying, "Why haven't you been able to provide me with a lion?"

After hearing this story, I said to Glen, "Now, tell me, what was your reason for not letting that man shoot a lion?" His answer was interesting. He said, "That man didn't deserve to shoot a lion."

He continued: "Anybody who loves wildlife and wild creatures must have an enormous respect for them, for the wildlife. They must have a tremendous respect for a lion, for a buffalo, for an elephant, or a leopard, and one has to be a good hunter to deserve to shoot one of those animals. That means not only being a good shot but also having the character of a good hunter. This man did not deserve to shoot a lion. He was a coward and a snob. So they drove him around in the hunting car and took his money from him. That was his punishment for not deserving to shoot a lion."

Chapter 7

Left in the Lurch in Sudan

When I recounted the story of my first safari with my eldest son, José, in Kenya in 1976, I mentioned that we were not able to hunt elephant because their hunting had just been banned. The following year, my friend Arturo Acevedo, who was always very much in love with elephants and the hunting of them, got news that there were some very good elephants on the eastern bank of the Nile River in the Sudan. Western bank elephants in Sudan were famous for their heavy ivory,

This is a group of curious but friendly villagers that we passed on our way from Juba to camp. Sudan.

but the hunter had to walk for perhaps a month to be able to find one because the country was so thickly forested; it was not good terrain for a short hunt. Arturo invited me to go with him to the eastern bank of the Nile, and to take another of my sons with me—Marcos, my second son. Arturo took his eldest son, Arturito, and Arturito's charming and sporty young wife, Teresa.

Arturito was going for twenty days. I had to cut my trip to fifteen days, because this took place during my second year as minister of economy; I couldn't be away for more than a couple of weeks. To get to the Sudan, one had to go through Nairobi and then take a small plane to the capital of Southern Sudan, which is Juba.

Sudan and Its People

Sudan is the largest country in Africa, covering about one million square miles on both sides of the River Nile. The country has some thirty million inhabitants in two distinct regions. The northern region is Arabic, the population there being Muslims. The main city in the north is Khartoum, which is the capital of the country. The southern region is completely different. The people in the south are blacks, and they account for about a third of the total population. Southern Sudanese are ethnically non-Arabs, as well as being among the oldest Christian groups known; some traditional African animistic beliefs are also practiced.

At this time the country had just gone through a bloody and lengthy civil war—the south against the north—sparked by feelings in the south that they were bullied by the north, by Khartoum, and didn't receive fair representation. The war had just ended, and, inasmuch as Sudan was famous for its good trophies—such as elephant, bongo, roan antelope, and lesser kudu—Arturo thought it would be a good idea to get in before anything else happened. The situation was still touchy.

So off we went. He would hunt with Glen Cottar and I with Peter Behr, my PH in Kenya. They had to travel by caravan from Nairobi to Sudan in trucks and Jeeps, taking

My son Marcos sitting on the top of the four-wheel-drive Suzuki so he can see over the tall elephant grass. Sudan.

every possible provision with them because there was nothing to be had in Sudan—not even food.

Travel Problems

My son and I flew from Buenos Aires by Swissair and arrived in Nairobi late at night. To our horror—this was the first bad omen of the hunt—although our rifle case came off the plane, our bags did not. We had packed all of the necessary hunting gear and equipment, in addition to special lightweight clothing designed for the hot and damp climate. We could not wait for our bags to be found, and so we spent the next day in Nairobi buying new gear. Swissair eventually paid us for our losses, but there were many items that could not be duplicated in Nairobi shops. We left the next day in a small plane.

Juba

The charter plane flew us to Juba, the capital of Southern Sudan. When we arrived Glen Cottar and my friend Arturo were there to meet us, their faces long and glum. I asked, "What's happened?" Glen told us that, as we already knew, for us to be able to hunt in Sudan, all the reservations for the concessions and the payment for the hunting blocks had to have been made through a Sudanese intermediary. Glen had complied with all of the restrictions and had paid the fees, but when we got there, the wildlife authorities knew nothing about it. The man he had dealt with turned out to be a crook. So there we were, with our safari caravan but no concession, no hunting block.

I had told Glen that, although I was minister of economy of Argentina, I had wanted to travel strictly incognito. But Glen soon informed me that if I didn't permit him to mention that I was a minister in Argentina, there would be no hunt. What could I do but agree? He proceeded, and made a good job of it.

At that time they were in the midst of elections in Sudan, and the only cabinet minister of the Southern Sudanese government in town was the minister of justice, who turned out to be a very nice man, educated at Harvard. The minister invited us to dinner at his home that evening, where we could also meet the head of the wildlife department. We had a very nice dinner in the garden, and, making the best of circumstances, I asked what Argentina might do for Sudan, perhaps in the area of agricultural livestock. Could we introduce new livestock breeds?

The minister's answer was surprising. He said, "Thank you very much, but there's nothing you can do. To begin with, for all our people, cows are a symbol of wealth. They don't kill a cow to eat its meat. Like the Masai, they have cows only to drink their blood or their milk, or for special ceremonies. They don't eat a cow. They buy their wives with so many cows. And the cattle are a status symbol."

So I asked, "Well, what about agricultural seeds, or something like that?"

"No, no. My people don't want agriculture, because they don't like to work with their hands. They are pastoralists. They look after their goats, sheep, and cattle, but they don't till the land."

The head of the wildlife department, however, understanding the difficulty of our situation despite our good faith efforts to play by the rules, drew a little map and showed Glen Cottar where we could go to hunt. It took us about a day and a half to drive there. We could not use the Toyota Land Cruisers, because the soil in that area was what they call cotton soil—very light, black soil into which a heavy vehicle will sink. So we had to use lightweight four-wheel-drive vehicles. These were small Suzukis into which we could barely squeeze ourselves, four people in each.

Stuck in the Mud

On the way to the hunting area we had to cross a lot of dry rivers. That is, they looked dry on top, but what we could see was only a crust. Underneath was a bog. Just as evening was

One of our trucks got stuck in the mud while we were crossing a riverbed on the way to our hunting area, and it had to be unloaded and dug out. My son Marcos is shown helping with the digging. Sudan.

approaching on the first day, our biggest truck got stuck in the mud crossing a river. As there was nothing we could do and it was getting dark, the crew simply unloaded it, and we had to spend the night there. Each of us slept outside, on a cot with a mosquito net. The next morning, when we awoke, we found around the cots the tracks of lions.

Maybe they hadn't been hungry, or maybe they thought I was too skinny. Arturo was plumper, but possibly he didn't smell good. They had walked around us and sniffed, but nobody heard a thing—not even the natives, who have sharp hearing.

In the morning, while the men were loading the truck, I went off to get a few photographs and to watch some local people who were washing their clothing in the river. So I crossed the river and then tried to cut back across at another point. There was a man there with his goats, and I took some pictures of him. And then, as I crossed, suddenly and to my horror, I flopped into the middle of the river.

I started to sink. Luckily, though, I had time to throw myself onto my back and give a shout. The man with the little herd of goats came up and gave me the end of his stick. I held on, and he pulled me out. If nobody had been there I'd have drowned for certain, because none of my party had seen or heard me. When I got back there was a big laugh on me, because I was covered with mud. My friends washed me off by throwing buckets of water over my head.

Friendly Villagers

After that we passed through many villages in which the people were all very friendly. In front of each was a young man with a spear, normally resting one foot on the other, as the Masai do, and looking after the goats or sheep or cows. The women were the ones who worked—chopping the wood or doing whatever had to be done. These people lived in little huts on stilts because of the floods. These were flood plains, and when the rains came they had to be up high to survive.

At one point on our journey overland I nearly got into trouble on account of my habit of taking photographs to later

One of the small villages we drove by on our way to our hunting area. Most of the mud and straw huts were built on stilts because of flooding during the rainy season. Sudan.

organize into a slide-video presentation. We had to cross Pibor Post, which could not be called a village but was a group of huts in which there was a sort of military checkpoint. While Glen was submitting our passports for inspection and explaining the purpose of our trip, I wandered off a little and attempted to take a few photos of the place. As soon as I got my small camera out there was a shout, and a soldier came running up and demanded that I give it to him. They were extremely sensitive to photos of a seemingly harmless nature, perhaps for military reasons. I was taken to the guard post, and after some explanation of my innocent intentions the incident concluded.

Trouble in Camp

On the following evening we got to the hunting area we had been looking for and pitched our camp just before sundown. We were just beginning to settle in when suddenly I heard shouting between Glen Cottar and somebody who

My son Marcos, in the front of the tent we shared at camp, preparing to wash and shave in the early morning. Sudan.

was speaking what sounded like Portuguese. After a time Glen came to fetch me and said, "Look, there's a Portuguese professional hunter here who says we are intruding on his concession. I can't understand him very well, but that's what I gather. As you speak Spanish, you can probably talk to him. Please come and help!" So I did.

At first this Portuguese, shouting very loudly, said that we were intruders—and all the rest one can imagine. I have learned that whenever somebody shouts at someone, the only way to stop him is to shout louder. So I did. In Spanish. And he understood perfectly. I said, "Look, I'm very sorry, but here's the map, here's the authorization, the written authorization we have from the head of the Wildlife Authority. We are not intruders. We are here legally. If the wildlife department has made a mistake, that is not our fault. We don't want to cause trouble, but that is the situation. We are not going to move. This is the place where the Wildlife Authority sent us."

Marmolín

It turned out that this man knew an Argentine who had worked quite a number of years in Sudan with hunting

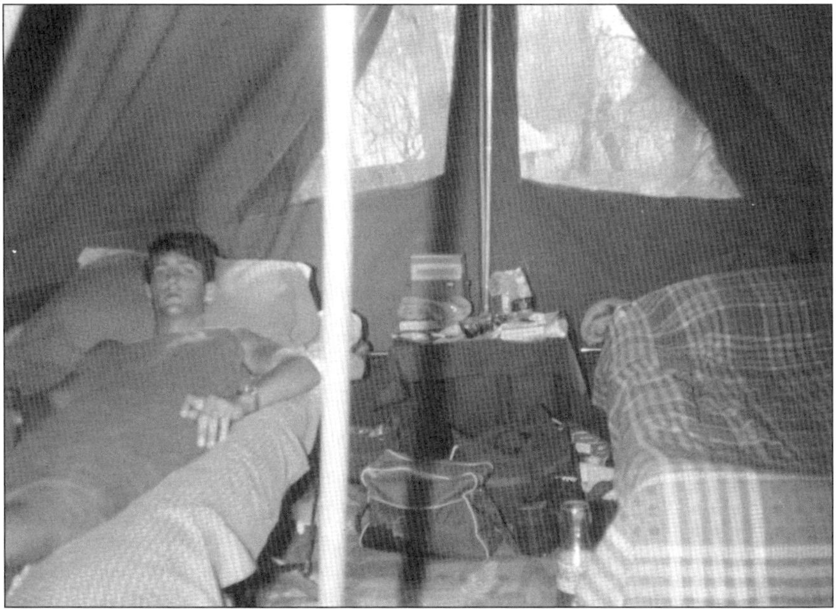

The damp heat was oppressive, so my son Marcos would wrap himself in a wet towel to get some rest on his cot in our small tent at camp. Sudan.

When one of our trucks got stuck in the mud in a riverbed on our way to the hunting area, we had to spend the night on our cots under the stars. Next morning we found lion tracks all around the cots. Sudan.

companies. When the Argentine died in a hospital, it was of an illness that couldn't be identified. Years afterward we thought it might have been one of the first cases of AIDS, because of what had happened to him. The Argentine's name was José Augusto Mármol, but everybody called him Marmolín. He was working for an outfitter, and one evening, driving the Jeep back to camp, he picked up a few local people who were asking for a ride. Going around a bend the vehicle bumped into a stone, and a young girl fell off and was rather badly hurt. She was taken to a hospital, and he was jailed.

Marmolín spent about a month in jail, and the stories he told about Sudanese jails were horrible. The prisoners were in a sort of dungeon, chained one to another, sitting on top of a sort of canal into which they had to urinate and do whatever else they had to do. They couldn't move. Fortunately, the hunting company and the Argentine consul finally got him out, but he must have caught AIDS there—or if it was not AIDS, whatever it was. A short time after he returned to the Argentine, he died.

When the Portuguese professional hunter gradually calmed down, I told him who I was, and at last he listened. I repeated our story about the map and the head of the wildlife department and said again that we were very sorry if we were unwittingly trespassing on his concession. But he also had to realize our plight: We Argentines had come all the way from Argentina and we had to find some solution to our problem. He couldn't just kick us out of the concession. Anyway, we wouldn't leave, because we thought we were within our rights, too. The story about Marmolín came in handy, because it created some sort of rapport between us; Marmolín was Argentine and I was Argentine, and this Portuguese PH had heard my name, probably through Marmolín.

I eventually was able to come to an agreement with him, that if he would show us which part of the concession would not obstruct his activities, we would stay there and be of no bother to him or his clients. The arrangement worked out pretty well. We even got to be on good terms, and I visited him and his American clients two or three times in the

I took this free-range springbok with Volker Grellmann. Damaraland area, Namibia.

I hunted this gemsbok (with Volker Grellmann) free range in the red, stony desert of Damaraland. Namibia.

I shot this roan antelope from a small herd on the eastern bank of the Nile River. Sudan.

White pelicans on Lake Nakuru. Together with the pink flamingoes, they make an impressive sight. Kenya.

With PH Neil Lindsay on the bank of the Zambezi River with the trophies of our hunt. Zimbabwe.

I was with Volker Grellmann when I took this southern greater kudu free range with a 400-yard shot. Namibia.

I shot this waterbuck on the bank of the Zambezi River. Matetsi area, Zimbabwe.

In the blind from where I shot my leopard with PH Neil Lindsay. Zimbabwe.

My son Marcos standing at the entrance of the valley where we waited for the venado *or mountain deer. Farther away is Pilicho Remy Solá. Province of Salta, Argentina.*

Camp at sunset on the magnificent Zambezi River. Matetsi area, Zimbabwe.

My son José and PH Peter Behr with my son's fringe-eared oryx. Lake Magadi area, Kenya.

With my son José in our first camp in the Loita Hills. This was my first safari in Africa. Masai Mara area, Tanzania.

Here I am with my first elephant, which I took with a side brain shot. Sundown in the Selous Game Reserve, Tanzania.

Giraffe in burnt grass. Selous Game Reserve, Tanzania.

My son Marcos, with PH Peter Behr, taking his Bright gazelle. Sudan.

evenings. Later on, he proved to be very useful to us with our trophies.

Hunting for our Trophies

Once we had got settled in, the first thing that Glen Cottar had on his mind was finding elephants for Arturo. So we went to the area where the elephants were supposed to be, but the only thing we saw were tracks—very big and lots of them. Glen estimated, looking at them in the light, fragile soil, that they had been there since December. This was February. It rains in December, and the dry season begins in January. When the water is gone, the elephants also leave. As a result, it seemed there was absolutely no chance of our finding them. (It's interesting to note, however, that exactly ten years later, in 1987, I went to Ethiopia for elephant. When I took my biggest elephant ever, an 85-pounder, it was just across the border from where I'd been in Sudan ten years earlier.)

My son Marcos and myself with the record-book lesser kudus we each took, one after the other. The government game scout is standing beside us. Sudan.

The tiang is a species of the Damaliscus family. Marcos is shown in the photo with the trophy he took. Sudan.

Having given up on elephant, we hunted eland, roan antelope (which is not found in many areas of Africa), and Bright gazelle, a subspecies of the Grant gazelle. I was very fortunate to take a very good Bright, and it still ranks number two in both the Rowland Ward and the Safari Club International record books.

Another interesting animal we hunted was the tiang. It is found mainly in Sudan and belongs to the *Damaliscus* family, as do the topi and the tsessebe. The horns of the tiang are not up to much, but they have a beautiful skin that is a sort of velvety, chocolate brown and a black face, shoulders, and hindquarters. The tiang makes a beautiful trophy. Like me, Marcos took both a tiang and a Bright gazelle. Then I took a roan antelope and he took an eland.

A Brace of Lesser Kudus

The really top trophy that we were after, however, was the lesser kudu. It is a very elusive animal and scarce, especially in Kenya, where most of the hunting was done for it in the past. Its senses of scent, hearing, and vision are all very well developed, and the animal can be difficult to find. The first time I read about the kudu was when I was in Kenya. I had taken with me

Hemingway's *The Green Hills of Africa*, the first of his books I ever read. In it, Hemingway speaks of his obsession with the kudu. He called it the "gray phantom" because it was so difficult to see, and he never got one, in spite of his obsession.

Here in Sudan there were lesser kudus, which are half the size of the greater kudu and even more rare; they are found only in a few small pockets in Africa. We really wanted one, but we had hunted almost to the end of our term and could not find any. One evening I went to my Portuguese friend, the PH, in a state of desperation and asked him if he could give me a tip where to find lesser kudus. He said, "Of course."

The next evening we followed his directions but saw nothing until we were just about to give up and go back to camp. Peter and I were ahead, and Marcos had gone back to the Jeep. Suddenly Peter said, "Stop, stop! Look, look!"

There were two lesser kudus, both very good—both record-book kudu. They were about three hundred yards away, but I had my .375 with me. I shot one through the shoulder and

The Bright gazelle is a subspecies of the Grant gazelle. I was fortunate in taking a trophy that still ranks second in both Rowland Ward's and Safari Club International's record books. Sudan.

watched it drop. The extraordinary thing was that its companion probably didn't hear the gun; in the forest the sound of shots gets drowned, and the other kudu simply stood there. I immediately ran back to the Jeep—it was about fifty yards off—got Marcos, pushed the rifle into his hands, and said, "Look, look! Quick, quick! Shoot at the middle of his shoulder! Look at that kudu!" Marcos did, and down came the second kudu.

Thus ended our Sudan hunt. In 1983 there was a renewal of civil war under the Sudanese People's Liberation Movement. The bitter fighting and widespread guerrilla activity ended any possibility of further safaris. A large proportion of the wildlife was killed for food, and the Sudan as a destination for sport hunting came to an unhappy end.

Before ending this chapter on the Sudan, I will tell a short and amusing anecdote. In the truck that brought up the foodstuffs and gear from Nairobi to Juba, the crew had brought some chickens and a cock, so that we could have fresh eggs and fowl. The cock crowed every morning, one or two hours before the time we had to get up, and everybody got to loathe it.

One day we had come back to camp at noon and were having our lunch outdoors when the cock came strutting by. My .458 was nearby, and Arturo asked me for a look at it. I handed it to him, and he loaded it with a single cartridge. He then pointed the .458 at the cock, which was only ten yards away, and fired. The cock simply disappeared. It was not an explosion. It was an implosion. All we ever found was one—exactly one—feather.

Chapter 8

Elephant Hunting in the Selous

Tanzania, formed by the union of Tanganyika and Zanzibar, came into being only in 1964. Tanganyika was the old German colony that saw so much fighting between the British and the Germans in World War I. It is also where Selous died. In the postwar peace treaties it was transferred to the United Kingdom and became a British colony. Britain gave the country its independence, or *uhuru* as they called it, in 1964, at more or less the same time as Kenya. Tanganyika then joined up with the island of Zanzibar, which had been famous for its slave and ivory trade. There was an important market for elephant tusks in Zanzibar, which had been a Portuguese colony in the sixteenth century and later an Arab sultanate. In 1890 it had become a British protectorate.

Tanganyika was quite as famous as Kenya for hunting; in fact, all of British East Africa was. Kenya, Tanganyika, and Uganda were the three countries that composed British East Africa, and that was where the safari industry began. The northern part of Tanganyika was in those days very similar to the southern part of Kenya, which is where we had hunted on our first African trip.

The Selous Game Reserve

Farther to the south is an area famous for its large herds of excellent elephant. That area of Tanzania is now called the Selous Game Reserve—the word *reserve* not meaning that you can't hunt there. To the contrary, the area is preserved for hunting. And that was where we were going.

The reserve was named in honor of Frederick Courteney Selous. Selous was a famous British hunter-explorer-naturalist who, although retired in England, immediately applied to join the army at the outbreak of World War I. He was sixty-three at the time. Although at first he was not accepted because of his age, Lord Kitchener himself authorized him to become intelligence officer to the Legion of Frontiersmen, later known as "the old and the bold." During the war their exploits made them famous.

Selous was British to the hilt, a man typical of Britishers of those days. At that time the head of the German army in Tanganyika, who led the famous native askari *Schutztruppe*, was General von Lettow-Vorbeck, an exceptionally good general and very Prussian in the old style. In January 1916 there was a battle on the Rufiji River in which the British were outnumbered by the Germans. Selous, who had been promoted to captain and awarded the D.S.O. (Distinguished

Moving camp in the Land Cruiser to cross the Selous from east to west in search of an area where I could hunt elephant.

Service Order), was very dashing and always at the front. He wore a big hunter's hat with a white hatband, and a German sniper shot him, putting a bullet through his head.

There was a furious reaction, because Selous was such an admired man. So great was the reaction that Von Lettow-Vorbeck sent a special letter expressing his condolences that such a man as Selous should have died under those circumstances. Selous's grave remains today right at the spot where he died, which is in the hunting reserve that was named after him. It is the best hunting area for elephant in Tanzania.

Tanganyika became independent in 1964, although it fell under communist influence when the Chinese built a railway to the north. They closed the country to hunting and tourism because they didn't want foreigners to see what was happening in it. Tanzania's first president, Julius Nyerere, was a Marxist-socialist, and he imposed a Marxist-socialist regime on the country, which became very poor compared with Kenya, which had not gone to the same extremes.

I remember my PH telling me that, when the hunting season was over, their job was to shoot wildlife to feed the population because there wasn't enough food for the people. There was no industry, no agriculture—nothing. Previously there had been a good tourist industry and a safari industry, with lodges like the one at Ngorongoro and elsewhere. But the communists put the idea into the heads of the natives that it was below their dignity to serve whites, and that was the end of that.

Then, perhaps ten or twelve years later, there was a change of policy. Nyerere was still president, but he realized that something had to be done. So they reopened hunting, including the Selous Reserve, which had suffered a lot as a result of poaching. The year I went with my friend Arturo Acevedo, 1984, it was just coming back. There weren't the same enormous elephants there used to be, but the possibility still existed of getting a good one.

Arturo arranged the safari, as he had done the one in Kenya. He knew the people in the wildlife department of Tanzania in Arusha. This time none of my boys were able to come with me, because they couldn't get away from their studies during the month of September. I was making the trip only for elephant.

Arturo took one of his sons, and I went alone. We met there, because I had arrived a week early to visit a few of the places I knew in Kenya that were now photographic safari locations. We met in Nairobi and then went on to Arusha in a small plane. Hunting was run by a state company called Tawico, the Tanzania Wildlife Corporation. It was tremendously inefficient, but there was nothing else. Arturo had been there before, however, and he knew a very good professional hunter who had been educated in a Portuguese mission. His name was Lazaro Massi, and he was very famous.

For my PH he had asked for Andrew Kissiri, who had been educated in a British mission. If Massi was the best available, Kissiri was the second best. One spoke Portuguese and the other perfect English. Kissiri was indeed a very good professional hunter. Of course, everything else was terrible. When we got

My seventy-pound tusker approaching on the sand river for its evening drink. Selous Game Reserve, Tanzania.

to camp the radio didn't work. They didn't have Toyota Land Cruisers. They did have British Land Rovers because there was a British assembly factory in Dar es Salaam.

The Selous Game Reserve is a little southwest of Dar es Salaam, which is on the coast of the Indian Ocean. So we had to get on a small charter plane and fly south from Arusha. We had different camps, and when I got to mine, Andrew Kissiri asked me what I wanted to hunt.

"What, don't you know? You're my professional hunter. They haven't told you?"

He said, "No, well, it happens that this is not my area. I hunt in the northern area, in the Masai area, but as you especially asked for me, Tawico assigned me to you."

"But didn't they give you my file to look at?"

"No, no. I've just read it this morning—that is, now."

I said I had come to hunt elephant.

"But this is not an elephant block. They have sent you to the wrong block. There are no huntable elephants in this block."

I nearly fainted. Luckily, my PH was a very alert and resourceful man, and also very intelligent.

"Look," he said, "Let's do one thing. This is a very nice area. You can see that there are herds of elephant, but none with any ivory worth shooting. You can see all sorts of animals here. We can drive around for two or three days, and in the meantime I'll try to get permission to move to a concession block where we can hunt elephants." So we did that, and it proved to be a very interesting and beautiful area.

A Buffalo Rodeo

I had told my PH that, although elephant was my reason for coming to Africa, I also wanted, if possible, to take a buffalo and a sable, that beautiful antelope. While we were touring around in the Land Rover, we saw an enormous herd of about three hundred buffalo. It was an impressive sight. Suddenly Andrew accelerated the vehicle to full speed and drove straight into the herd. He began to work the herd like cows in a rodeo, trying to put some to one side and others to another. I didn't know what

Elephant cow with small calf at foot sucking up water from a sand river after drilling a hole through the sand with its trunk. Selous Game Reserve, Tanzania.

he was doing, so I grabbed my camera and began taking pictures. Suddenly he stopped. Fifty yards away, to the left, was standing a very good buffalo bull.

"There's your buffalo," said Andrew. "Shoot. From the car."

"No."

They had passed me my .375.

I said, " I want to shoot a buffalo on foot. I want to walk after him." I made a noise, and the buffalo went off.

A Double Nitro Express

I got down and asked for my double rifle. On my first African safari I hadn't had a double rifle. Glen Cottar obtained one for me before my trip to the Sudan, but I was never able to use it there. When hunting was banned in India, all the double Express rifles, of which the maharajahs had enormous collections, became useless, and they all came onto the market. Many of them found their way into Africa. Kynoch, the famous cartridge factory, closed for lack of demand, and only guns that had cartridges left over were of any use. In any case, the fashion for the double Nitro Express rifle was past.

Glen had told me all about this, and I had said, "Well, if you have the chance of getting one, send me a telegram and buy one for me. I'd like a .470." Arturo had a .500, which was too heavy for me, and I thought that a .470 would be just the thing. In August, six months after our first Kenya safari, I got a telegram from Glen Cottar to tell me that he had found a very good Rigby double Express .470 with two hundred Kynoch cartridges.

"Do you want it?"

I immediately replied, "Yes," and he bought it for me at a price that today would be considered low. This would be my first occasion to use it. I had never shot with it before, and I was longing to try it out. I ended up shooting all my elephant and buffalo with it. It was a wonderful side-by-side rifle, much like a shotgun and great fun to hunt with.

So I got down from the vehicle and walked around to the back, where the gun case was. I said, "Get out my double and let's walk after that buffalo."

We did, but by then, of course, it had left. When we got back to the car Andrew, my PH, said, "Please excuse me, but I didn't know the sort of hunter you are. So many people, if they want a good buffalo and have a chance of shooting one from the car, will do so. Please excuse me. I didn't know you well enough." I suppose I could have easily taken that buffalo, the one that got away. But what is the fun of shooting a standing buffalo from a hunting car?

Another Word about My Double

I wrote to Rigby about my double, and they had its number on record. The gun had changed hands various times since it had left Britain. My double had been made in the pre–World War II period, and the cartridges contained cordite, which had been a big improvement over the earlier black gunpowder.

At the end of the nineteenth century the frontier wars in the United States were fought with the famous Remingtons and Winchesters, which were breach rifles, but the big African

Members of our hunting team drinking water in a sand river from a hole drilled by elephants and enlarged by the men. Selous Game Reserve, Tanzania.

guns at the time still used black powder until the time when cordite replaced it. Cordite was a good choice for tropical countries, because it could stand the heat well and did not produce excessive pressure in the barrels. Nowadays, of course, cordite has disappeared, having been replaced by modern gunpowders.

I was delighted to have obtained this double with its ammo. It will last for all my lifetime and the next generations as well. One doesn't shoot many times from a double rifle.

Elephants in the Selous

We drove around for three or four days, watching and photographing all sorts of animals. At one point my PH showed me how an elephant herd drinks from sand rivers. What they do is use their trunk as if it were a drill—almost as if they were drilling for oil. They bore through the sand and then suck up the water and put it into their mouths. A female with a small calf will push the water through her trunk into the mouth of the calf. I got some pictures of that. Although I was not able to hunt during those three or four days, it was fascinating to observe the animals and the land.

The Selous Hilton

After the fourth day, Andrew said, "Well, now I know where we should go. We've got to cross almost the whole of the Selous Reserve, which is very big. We have to cross it from east to west and find this place where I have obtained permission." The Selous game reserve covers 54,000 square kilometers, or more than 20,000 square miles.

So everything was packed into the Land Rover and off we went. We drove and drove and drove. The Selous Reserve is mostly forest, and many times there were fallen trees blocking the way that had to be cut. There were no roads at all, and the men had to open a track for the vehicle.

At the end of the first day Andrew said, "I think we've lost our way." (There was no GPS in those days.) We should have arrived at our destination, but we hadn't. So we spent the night. The evening temperatures were very mild, and I came to think of this as my evening at the Selous Hilton.

The accommodations proved very good. We had dinner around the campfire, which is always nice. Only Andrew and I could speak English, but I could speak a few words of Swahili to the men. We got to talking, telling stories under the moon and stars, and then it was off to bed without blankets. They didn't even bother to pitch a tent. It was one of the nicest nights that I have had in Africa.

As always the best food, if one has shot anything, is antelope meat. Well, we did shoot one. There were quite a few Lichtenstein hartebeest about, and Andrew at some point had said, "Let's shoot one for camp meat." There is an allowance for shooting a certain amount for the pot. I shot one, and in addition to being toothsome it turned out to be a very good trophy. Its horns hang on my trophy room wall.

The next day we continued on. The problem was to keep the water fresh. The canteens were plastic, and if one went out in the morning with a canteen of water, two hours later it was hot.

Drinking hot water makes one feel like vomiting. But I found the answer: Fill the canteen with tea. If the tea gets cold, it doesn't matter—it's cold tea. Or it can be warm tea, or lukewarm tea. But it's never hot water. This was a trick I learned in the Sudan.

Anyway, after that wonderful night at the Selous Hilton we never found the area Andrew was looking for, although we did arrive at my friend Arturo's camp. It had taken us three days to drive across the Selous Reserve. When we arrived at Arturo's camp, he was surprised to see us.

We put our camp alongside his, but the problem was that we couldn't hunt there because we would be in his way. We had to go out of his area to look for animals, and it was a long drive every day. That was inconvenient because of the time lost, but at least we had a good camp, friends to come back to, and a meal and a whiskey at night around the campfire.

Arturo Acevedo

This was to be my last safari with Arturo Acevedo, whom I respected a great deal. Arturo, who was a little older than I, died in 1999. When he was very young he had contracted polio, and it had affected his spine. As a result he walked with a limp and could not stand very straight. He was also a little bit hunchbacked. But he had taken up hunting to prove that with courage and willpower you can do anything, whatever your disabilities. Arturo and I were second cousins, but the friendship that arose through our mutual love for Africa and hunting was our strongest bond.

Hunting Elephants in the Selous

We went out every day with my PH searching for elephant. We saw perhaps a hundred of them outside of Arturo's area, and we always walked up to them. That was a great experience. The country was thick and bushy with forest, and we couldn't see their tusks from a distance—so we had to walk up to them.

The elephant is shortsighted. It has very bad eyesight but good hearing and a wonderful sense of smell. I remember that once while we were looking at a herd drinking water from

Sitting in the sand river the morning after I shot my first elephant. Selous Game Reserve, Tanzania.

a sand river they got a whiff of us. Up went their trunks like periscopes, turning round and round.

When that periscope goes up, beware. If an elephant gets one's wind it will either run away or, if alarmed, charge. The problem with the wind in Africa is that it continually changes. It swirls. Normally the PH will have a cigarette in his hand when getting near an animal to see which way the smoke goes. If he doesn't smoke he'll kick the earth or have a little pouch with ashes to throw into the breeze. The danger is that if the wind swirls or changes as one is getting near an elephant, it could mean trouble.

Andrew Kissiri took me almost close enough to the elephants to touch them. The first time one gets near an animal that is nine to twelve feet high and weighs five to six tons, one feels rather like David before Goliath. The first time one goes up to a mammoth like that one feels something—at the very least, awe. One has to look at both sides, because many times elephants will have only one good heavy tusk, having broken off the other. Some people have shot elephants thinking they are shooting a good one and obtained only one tusk. But looking at both sides is an additional risk.

With Andrew we inspected about a hundred elephants, but none were good enough. One day we did shoot a very nice sable, however, a beautiful antelope with glossy black hide, scimitarlike horns, and white on its face like a clown. It is one of the most important trophies in the antelope group. The sable is a cousin of the roan antelope, which I had taken in Sudan. I had said, "Elephant first," but then, when I saw a sable herd, it was, "Let's try to get our sable." We did, but then I had only two or three days left for my hunt. From Tanzania I was flying straight to New York for a meeting of the Group of Thirty,* of which I was a member.

Andrew was also getting concerned. At that time in Tanzania there were some oil explorations going on, and one of the members of his team remembered spotting elephant nearby. The place was about an eight-hour drive away, though, and we had only three days left. He said, "Let's go and set up a fly camp." So we did, arriving in late afternoon, near sundown.

There was a very good sand river there, with a pool that the elephants had probably dug up. An elephant herd was drinking. We stood behind some trees on a little hill and looked them over. There was no bull with more than sixty pounds of ivory per side. Nowadays sixty pounds is quite a good tusk, but in those days it was sort of, as the English say, *infra dig* (beneath one's dignity) to shoot a sixty-pounder.

Arturo had told me that he had never shot an elephant with tusks under eighty pounds. Andrew, my PH, asked me, "Well, what's your limit?"

"I'd love to have anything over eighty. But, as we're getting to the last two days, I'll settle for anything over seventy," I said.

**The members of the Group of Thirty are personalities from all over the world: economists, financial specialists, academics, businessmen, and former government officials. Membership is by special invitation only, and the group meets every six months, rotating between the United States and Europe. The group publishes brochures and does studies on economic and financial matters.*

So we waited. And late in the day, nearly at sundown, we suddenly saw an old elephant come walking in to drink. Obviously it was not a member of the herd. It was an old elephant that had been kicked out of the herd, too old to be reproductive. It was coming in for its evening drink. The others had almost finished.

Andrew said, "There's your elephant. But wait. The herd has nearly finished drinking. We can't go in and shoot him in the herd. If we shoot in the middle of the herd we can get into trouble."

He was patient enough to restrain me. Of course, I was ready to go straight at the elephant.

We waited until the old bull was alone. Then Andrew said, "Now," and we got up. Unfortunately, there was no one to take photos of the stalk; my sons had done that job in the past. I took my double and we went into the long grass. Crouching, we walked up to within twenty-five yards of the elephant. The wind was in our favor, and it never knew we were there.

The Brain Shot

The best shot to take at an elephant is a brain shot. If one succeeds, the elephant falls like a stone. But the brain is very small.

I measured it afterward and have photos. From the side, the target area is only seven inches by seven inches. It's a very small brain in the middle of a very big head. The rest of the elephant's head is like a honeycomb. It's not solid bone—probably that would make it too heavy.

The first man to discover this was the famous Karamojo Bell, the notorious ivory hunter at the end of the nineteenth century and beginning of the twentieth who shot about a thousand elephants for their ivory. He was very friendly with a chief of the Karamojo tribe, in the north of Kenya and Uganda. Everybody at that time used to shoot at the elephant's body—ten shots, eleven shots, whatever it took. Finally the elephant went down, if it didn't get away.

This tribesman opened an elephant's head for Bell and showed him where the brain was. It was as if it were hung midway on a stick between the two ear holes. If one has a side shot, the place to aim is about four inches along a line from the ear to the eyes. If one is above or below, ahead or behind, one must calculate the angle of penetration.

As for a frontal shot, some people will say that if the elephant is charging or facing the hunter, he must aim at the second wrinkle at the top of the trunk. But that is not correct. To begin with, the distance to the elephant makes quite a difference to the angle of the shot. And also, a man is small compared with an elephant. He has to shoot upward to get to the brain. One must look at the ears and imagine that the brain is in the middle of a line between the ear holes. Whatever the position of the head, one has to go for the middle of the head, the place between the ear holes—not the eyes, not the trunk, not the wrinkles of the trunk. Nothing but that.

Of course a heart or lung shot is also good, but the best is a brain shot. It is considered the most difficult shot to place, and few professional hunters will let a hunter try for it if they don't know how he shoots. But really it's the easiest shot—if, that is, one knows where to place it and how to handle the gun. This was my first experience, but I had read a lot about it, especially from Karamojo Bell's memoirs.

When we got up to this elephant it was in the bed of the river, and we were more or less on a level with it. As a result, I didn't have the problem of angling my shot upward. I had to place the bullet at precisely four inches from the ear in the direction of the eye, and there were only a few seconds in which to do it: I was crouching in long grass and had to approach to within twenty or twenty-five yards and stand up to fire. As soon as one moves or stands, the elephant may catch the movement.

Bringing the double up to the shoulder is like shooting a shotgun. The gun must go immediately into position. Well, I did it, and I was lucky enough to do it right. I was amazed. The elephant fell like a house of cards. That enormous beast simply crumpled. A moment later Andrew

Thanks to PH Andrew Kissiri's good advice, I was able to take my first elephant. Selous Game Reserve, Tanzania.

came running up and congratulated me, saying that I had taken a seventy-pounder. Wonderful, I said. I never knew it was so easy.

The Night of the Elephant

After that everything was wonderful. The sun was setting, so there was time for only a few photos. It was too late to get the tusks out. We spent the night by the side of the sand river, and I didn't even put my small tent up, the weather being so mild. We had a big celebration with all of the boys. They had their beer, I had my whiskey, and I couldn't have been happier. I had taken my first elephant with a neat brain shot. We called it "the night of the elephant."

The next morning we went down to the elephant, and the team began hacking it up to get out the tusks. About a fourth to a third of the length of the tusks is inside the head: That part is hollow and holds the nerve. Obviously, if that hollow section is longer than expected, the weight of the tusk may be lower than estimated. The crew also removed the four feet for stools. Elephant skin is very thick, about four or five inches, and is usable only from the middle of the body down, although the skin of the ears and trunk is also good. I have belts, shoes, and a wallet made of elephant skin, and I had some handbags made for my wife, daughter, and daughters-in-law. It's very strong and gets supple with use. The natural color is gray, although some people will dye it black or brown. I like the natural color.

I asked the crew to open up the head of the elephant. I wanted to see the exact position of the brain, and I got photos of it from a side view. It's like a little sausage, right in the middle of the head. It was amazing to see—and just as Karamojo Bell had described.

While the boys were hacking up the elephant other elephants appeared. They came around to have a look. They didn't bother us. They just wanted to see what was happening and walked off.

An elephant's meat is as tough as can be, but the Africans get inside the carcass and hack it all out until nothing is left. It's the drums of the forest that bring them. Word gets around, and you soon see people from the nearby villages. There weren't very many villages here, but people seemingly arrived from nowhere and crawled inside the elephant. They left the carcass stripped of meat and carried away every last bit.

Of course, the first thing one does after having shot an elephant is to cut off its tail. That is a tradition that goes back to the old days. When the old ivory hunters were out hunting elephant, they didn't have much logistical support. They probably went on to hunt another elephant, and then another, finally returning to take the tusks after the meat around them had rotted a bit. But the hunter immediately cut off the tail, as a sign that the carcass had an owner. It meant that nobody could touch that elephant. To this day, one keeps the tails. I've got all my tails at home.

Andrew's estimate proved correct. We weighed the tusks when we got back to camp, and they were seventy pounds each. Of course, they were weighed officially afterward.

The conical nerve is taken out of the hollow base of the elephant's tusks that is inside the head of the elephant. Selous Game Reserve, Tanzania.

Around the campfire we had another good celebration, with Arturo and the rest of the party.

The End of the Safari

The next morning I had to leave. On our way back to the airstrip, on the other side of the Selous, I asked Andrew if we had time to hunt a buffalo. Fortunately we did, and I took a good one with my .470 Rigby double. It was in a fairly large, moving herd, and the hunt for it was exciting. So I ended up the safari with my first elephant and my second buffalo, as well as my first sable antelope. I was very pleased.

Chapter 9

Mongol Heights and the Rebellious Interpreter

After my first few safaris in Africa, I wanted to diversify my hunting destinations. I had heard friends speak of the extraordinary rams of Mongolia. These animals were said to be enormously large—the biggest wild rams in the world. I had heard too that they are very difficult to hunt, and for two reasons: first, finding them; and second, the physical exertion necessary at 13,500 to 15,000 feet where the air is thin and breathing is difficult.

Genghis Khan and a Brief History of Mongolia

Mongolia is an ancient country. It covers about 932,056 square miles, making it a little larger than Alaska, and has a population of around 1.5 million. It shares borders with China and Russia (Siberia).

In the twelfth century, Genghis Khan's ambitions brought him and his Mongols, or Tartars, onto the stage of history. Genghis Khan, or Chingis Khan, succeeded his father at the age of thirteen as chieftain in a remote part of northeastern Mongolia. He gradually expanded his domain, and by the beginning of the thirteenth century, at which time he was forty, he and his fierce warriors had conquered most of the land from China to Persia and the Caspian Sea—that is, the whole breadth of Asia.

Genghis Khan began his campaign by acquiring allies and subordinate states, which were called khanates, and skillfully

These two Mongolians at the airport are in their traditional attire, called Del. *It includes a long high-collared tunic that falls below the knees, buttons down the side, a colorful sash, boots, and a western-style felt hat. Ulan Bator, Mongolia.*

using the art of power politics. His original capital was at Karakoram. China, although an empire and very large, was weak because it lacked a strong central authority and because real power was divided.

The Mongols were great horsemen on their small but sturdy horses, and they were famous as mounted warriors. Their battles were notoriously bloody, and after they had conquered a village or town they generally exterminated without pity everybody in it that was not useful to them. On horseback they were unstoppable, and people were terrified of them.

When Genghis Khan died at the age of sixty-five while hunting, he left four sons among whom he divided his territory in four khanates. They continued his exploits, going as far off as Russia and setting fire to Moscow in the mid-thirteenth century. His grandson Kublai Khan, after defeating his brothers, turned his attention to the east and effectively dominated all of China, moving his capital from Karakoram to Peking and establishing the Yuan Dynasty by the end of the thirteenth century.

In the west the Tartars, as they called them in Russia, established themselves in the Crimea. They formed a khanate, conquered Kazan on the Volga, and again took and set fire to Moscow after a tremendous massacre. Ivan the Great finally stopped them. Later they were annexed by the Turks and the Russians. Nowadays Crimea forms part of Ukraine, although its population remains ethnically and religiously more related to the Turks.

Karakoram was in the north-center of what is now Mongolia, not far from the present capital of Ulan Bator. After Kublai Khan the Mongol empire gradually crumbled because of internal strife and pressure from the Russians to the west and the Manchus to the east. China, after regaining its independence, ultimately ruled Mongolia for about three centuries. In the early twentieth century Mongolia regained its independence, although it remains torn between Russia and China. Their capital was called Urga (now Ulan Bator), located more or less in the center of what was called Outer Mongolia. And there was an Inner Mongolia inside the Chinese empire.

After the Russian revolution of 1917, a Peoples' Republic of Mongolia was established with Russian help, and the capital was renamed Ulan Bator, which means "Red Hero." Twenty years of purges and slayings to impose communism and erase Buddhism, although costing a large number of lives, were not successful at eliminating the tradition and pride of ancestry of the Mongolians. Less than 5 percent of the population joined the Communist Party, and in spite of Soviet opposition, in 1962 the Mongolians held a massive celebration of the 800th anniversary of the birth of Genghis Khan. They hate both Russians and Chinese alike, because when the great Mongol empire declined in strength and importance it became a puppet of first one and then the other. But the country never lost its traditions or its pride.

When one visits Mongolia and sees their big temples, which are Buddhist, one realizes that in their faith and their ethnic composition the people are nearer to the Chinese than to the Caucasians or Eurasians. That was the experience of the famous Venetian traveler Marco Polo, who first brought news of the Mongols to Europe. He traveled as a merchant along the famous Silk Road to the East.

Marco Polo

Marco Polo spent fifteen years in the court of Kublai Khan in the thirteenth century. When he returned to the West he brought with him several important discoveries. In addition to silk, for example, there was gunpowder. There were instruments, such as the compass. And he also brought back word of enormous sheep or rams. He never saw any, but he did see some horns picked up from dead rams; they were enormous. He brought the information back to the European courts, but of course they didn't believe him. Not very many years later, however, a Franciscan monk who returned from Mongolia to Europe did bring a set of horns back with him—and then they believed. Travel, however, was difficult.

Very late in the nineteenth century, an Englishman by the name of St. George Littledale traveled with his wife and a very small party to Mongolia. He shot quite a few of those large sheep, called argalis, and was the first European in modern times to bring back their heads, taking them to the famous London taxidermist Rowland Ward. Later St. George Littledale and Russian prince Demidoff went on another such expedition, and the latter wrote a book called *After Wild Sheep in the Altai and Mongolia*.

The Big Rams or Argalis of Mongolia

The biggest of these big rams are the Altai argali. The Altai is the range of mountains on Mongolia's northwest border with Russia. The highest part of the range is toward the north, and that's where the biggest rams live. They are called the high Altai argalis. Farther to the south the rams in the mid-Altais are smaller in size, and much farther down is the Gobi Desert; Gobi argalis are the smallest.

The Latin name for them is *Ovis ammon ammon*. *Ovis* means sheep and *ammon ammon* comes from the Egyptian god Ammon, the king of the gods—that's because this is the king of sheep. The biggest rams are the size of a small pony, being about four feet at the shoulders. That's big for a ram.

I'm looking rather tired the evening we came back from a fly camp after a week of unsuccessful hunting and mountain climbing. This was my tent, a yurt, at base camp. Mongolia.

The heads alone are very large: When I weighed mine after it was cut off I found that it weighed 55 pounds; the rams weigh about 440 pounds. The males of course are much bigger than the females, and their horns are thicker and longer.

Argalis have very long legs, which are useful for climbing the enormous mountains they live among. Their horns are very thick at the base, with a circumference of about twenty inches; they curl outward like a corkscrew. Measured along the curl, the big ones measure more than sixty inches.

Second in size is the Marco Polo ram. Their horns are a little flatter on top and extend out farther than those of the Altai argali. Its Latin name is *Ovis ammon poli,* in honor of Marco. Ovis Ammon is the family name. And there are about ten subspecies, the last name of which identifies them according to the region or the name of their discoverer.

One of the most famous territories for these argalis, especially the Marco Polo, is the Pamir Mountains, where four countries meet: Afghanistan, Pakistan, China, and Russia. There is an enormous plateau in the Pamir Mountains surrounded, of course, by high peaks, and that is one of the special regions for these animals. Bert and Chris Klineburger led an expedition into Afghanistan and the Wakhan Corridor in 1967, taking Marco Polo and opening the area for modern sportsmen. When the Russians invaded Afghanistan toward the end of 1979, that closed the country. And China was closed for years to all foreigners. There is a very interesting book on the opening of China in modern times entitled *China Safari*, written by Robert Lee, the explorer and international hunter who owns the Hunting World shop in New York. His exploits were truly remarkable.

Russia was also closed in 1890, but they gave special authorizations to some hunters, such as St. George Littledale. He received special permission from the Russian government. And afterward, in later years, there were various famous international hunters such as Major Cumberland, Elgin Gates, James Clark, Bill Morden, and the two sons of Teddy Roosevelt, Kermit (who went with his father on his African safari) and his brother Theodore Jr. They both hunted the argali in Mongolia.

My Trip to Mongolia

Three years after my Tanzania safari, in 1987, I was able to arrange a Mongolian hunt through the same outfitter that had organized my safari in Tanzania. The founder of Safari Outfitters, Roman Hupalowski, had died and been succeeded by a younger man from Wyoming called Lloyd Zeman, a great sheep hunter who unfortunately was killed a few years later when his horse fell over a cliff in Wyoming. Safari Outfitters and the Klineburgers were the two big U.S. outfitters that opened up hunting in Russia and Asia to the Western world, but at that moment, with Russia closed, the only place to go for argali was Mongolia.

In 1987 it was not possible to hunt a Marco Polo. Nowadays things are different. The big fashion is to hunt for Marco Polo in former Soviet states that are now independent, especially Tajikistan and Kirghizistan. It's actually much more expensive to hunt for Altai argali now in Mongolia than it was in my time, because they have become scarcer. The Marco Polos, on the other hand, have become more popular and abundant.

Argalis have two predators. Wolves are the more serious of the two, attacking young lambs and females, and one finds many dead animals killed by wolves. And of course the locals hunt sheep for food if they can. I don't think they would take a big ram, however, as it is easier to kill ewes or lambs.

In some periods the argalis, because they were difficult to find, have been considered an endangered species. But in reality, when people have gone and explored for them, they have found large numbers. They are difficult to find because their territory is so vast, both in Mongolia as well as China and Siberia. It has been their isolation that has helped them to survive.

The camp manager's wife in my yurt at base camp. She cooked for me and tended the stove for heating the big tent. Mongolia.

Group of nomad pastoralists moving their camp to a new pasture with their camels and small horses. Mongolia.

Hunting for argali begins in summer—that is, July—when their coat is fawn to reddish. Then, as the seasons change, their coat gradually gets grayer; it changes to blend into the color of the landscape. When there is snow on the ground in November, which is about the last month in which they can be hunted, they become nearly white. Some hunters think it best to go in November because at that time of year the snow brings the animals down from the mountains. Others say July is best, because then you're first in.

Be that as it may, my hunt was in the month of September, which is halfway through the hunting season. In those days all hunts were arranged by the official tourist agency of Mongolia, Zhuulchin. But I had organized mine through Safari Outfitters and Lloyd Zeman, who had a quota of just so many hunters he sent to Zhuulchin each year under his patronage. Zhuulchin did the rest.

At that time I also had received an invitation from an Austrian friend of mine to hunt chamois in Austria. I had to go to Europe anyway, because I had a meeting there; I always tried to intertwine business with hunting. Going first to Austria to hunt my chamois was an advantage, because from Vienna I could take an Aeroflot Russian plane to Moscow and from there get on an Aeroflot Tupolev to Ulan Bator. There was no other way to reach Ulan Bator in those days.

The Vienna-to-Moscow leg was probably a three-hour flight, but then from Moscow to Ulan Bator took eleven hours, with two stops for refueling—one in Omsk and the other in Irkutsk. They made the passengers wait for an hour on the ground during each stop. Fortunately, I had been warned not to travel in economy class on an Aeroflot Tupolev because it was like a chicken coop, with children and animals crawling everywhere. Even first class wasn't very good by our standards, but it was bearable.

I was concerned that my rifle and bags be taken off the plane from Vienna and put onto the right plane to Ulan Bator. A friend of mine had once told me that he had arrived at Ulan Bator without his rifle. He had had to wait a week to get it. One had only fifteen days in which to hunt, so I put a lot of pressure on the flight attendants, asking them five times if the rifles had been transferred to the right plane. At last, all was ready.

This time I was traveling alone. None of my friends could make the trip at this time of the year, so I had decided to go by myself. It's not the best way to travel. Anything might happen, and to be there with a friend is always preferable. But I didn't want to lose the chance. Who knows when another would come along?

On my plane, however, were many other hunters. There were Spaniards, Austrians, Germans, and Americans. They could all be recognized by the way they dressed. Those from the United States dressed in hunting clothes or camouflage. The ones from Austria and Germany wore their typical green Alpine hats and short pants, or lederhosen. And the Spaniards wore clothes more or less like the Austrians. I was the only one not dressed in hunting clothes. I intended to change once I got there.

When one arrives in Ulan Bator, as in all developing countries, going through customs is generally a mess. I had to find my interpreter, and the whole thing was truly chaotic. Everybody was speaking at once and bustling around in disarray. Zhuulchin, the official agency, assigns an interpreter to each hunter who will take him where he has to go and accompany him on the hunt. When they had asked me what language I spoke, I had told them English and Spanish. They had only one interpreter in Spanish, and they had thought fit to give him to me. There was, however, a Spanish hunter who sat beside me on the plane who spoke very bad English. He was furious because I got the Spanish interpreter, while he got a person who spoke only poor English, like himself.

My interpreter found me easily, probably because I was the only hunter that wasn't dressed like the others. And, of course, I looked foreign to him—that is, I wasn't a Mongol. The interpreter immediately introduced himself to me. He was a young man who had studied the Spanish language for four years at the university in Cuba. He was very able and immediately got me through customs; I would never have

Our fly camp at an altitude of 15,000 feet. I slept alone in the small tent. The Mongols of my hunting party slept outside under the stars in their big cloaks. It was very cold. Mongolia.

got through without his help. Then he took me to the hotel, called the Ulan Bator Hotel, an enormous building and typical of what is found in Russian communist countries. Everything was on a big scale, and the bedroom was immense. The hotel's porter was very elegant in his traditional dress. They try to imitate the civilized way of doing things that they have seen in the West.

That afternoon we made a tour of the city and visited all the public monuments and public buildings. All of them were enormous: big buildings, a big theater, big meeting places, a big statue of the liberator of Mongolia. In the museum there was a huge mounted Altai argali that made my mouth water.

Off to the High Altai

The next day we left in a terrible turboprop plane from Ulan Bator for a small town called Hovd, where we had to meet the camp manager who was coming to fetch us in a four-wheel-drive vehicle. Now, again, the interpreter was very useful, because there were no seat assignments for the plane. When the time came to board there was a rush and scramble to get in, and some people got left out. We were first in, thanks to my interpreter.

Traveling by air to the town of Hovd, to the west of Ulan Bator at the foothills of the Altai mountain range, took about four hours. Upon arrival we went to the small local hotel, where we spent the night. And there I met the head of our camp, who, although he must have been younger than me, looked much older. He had the wrinkled, weather-beaten, and leathery face one sees in people who live in cold climates and strong winds. We sat around a table in the hotel with him and made plans. There were two animals I could hunt: One was the high Altai ram, because I had chosen the top of the range, where one finds the biggest specimens. The other was the Siberian ibex.

I found the hotel in Hovd pleasant enough; there were hostesses dressed up in the local fashion. I noticed some big tin cans there that looked like the kind that in olden times the milkman used to drive around with. I asked what was in them. It proved to be mare's milk—milk from a female horse. Fortunately I had heard some stories about it and didn't drink. There was a big ladle, and I sipped a tiny bit and pretended to drink, only to be polite. But I had heard that the man who had been to the same camp where I was going, the president of an important bank in Alaska, had let himself be convinced to drink mare's milk. He got such severe diarrhea that he couldn't go hunting, and he lost his chance to get an argali. I didn't make the same mistake.

The next day we were off in a Russian 4x4, one of those made by Fiat in Russia. It was very good, and excellent for hilly and bumpy tracks. The drive lasted about eleven hours. It was a very long trip, but it gave me a chance to acclimatize gradually as we gained altitude. That was a good thing, because our base camp was at an altitude of twelve thousand feet.

On the way there, it was interesting to see various settlements or camps. The Mongols are nomad pastoralists, so they live in camps with tents, those big white, round, felt tents they call yurts. They are sustained by long poles, and there is normally a whole cluster of them. The Mongols raise horses, goats, sheep, and yaks. The yak is a bovine that looks like a cross between a horse and a cow. It can be ridden like a horse and can pull a cart. The females can be milked. The yak is a big, shaggy animal that weighs about a metric ton, or 2,200 pounds, and has a shoulder height of up to six feet.

The terrain we passed was very barren, with very poor vegetation. The Mongols also have camels, and when they move to a new pasture they fold up their tents and let the camels carry the poles. A camp on the move is an interesting sight. The whole family moves together like a tribe, with some on horseback and some on camels.

I found the Mongols to be a very friendly people. They have a special drink that they like, a sort of Mongolian vodka, which is rather sweet. My interpreter had told me to carry a few bottles to use if we had to celebrate with the team when I got my argali. But I had to hide them prior to that, because Mongolians are not used to having strong alcohol. If they drink they get dead drunk, and that would be the end of hunting for the next day. In addition we had what one always takes on such trips: packs of Camel cigarettes as presents or tips for the men and sweets for the children. Theirs is not a monetary economy, so money doesn't mean much to them. Camel cigarettes and sweets for the children mean more to them than money.

Hunting from Base Camp and Fly Camp

The yurt I was assigned had a stove in the middle. Normally the stove is heated with yak dung, which consumes itself very quickly. But fortunately the men had brought a big log along, as there was no firewood in the area. Pieces of this log were chopped off daily for my stove. The camp manager, who was the number one professional hunter, came and introduced his wife to me. She was the one who tended the stove. She told me not to get up in the morning before she came and heated the tent by lighting the stove with wood. Once it got warm, I was to get up.

The evenings were very cold—about four degrees below zero Fahrenheit. The problem with that was the toilet. In Africa the camp toilets are only a few yards away from one's tent, and the climate is mild. But here the toilet was fifty yards up the mountainside. That's a long way when it's twenty below. The other problem was that I had been told not to bring my own sleeping bag. So I didn't. After the first night I awoke in the morning with red bites, thanks to somebody who had been in those sheets before me. They hadn't changed them. I immediately asked for a change of sheets and got them. One must always take one's own sleeping bag.

The next morning we started off to explore the area for two or three days on horseback. These were little pony-horses, the same size as the ones in the prints of Genghis Khan and his warriors. They're very good and strong, being especially good at climbing. They are a bit vicious, however, and try to bite one's toe when the foot goes into the stirrup.

Spending the first three days on horseback was helpful because it allowed me to acclimatize a little more to the altitude. After those three days we went farther afield on horseback, and when we got to a place where the guides thought there might be argalis, we got off and glassed. We spent hours glassing. Fortunately I had taken along a powerful spotting scope, a 60X, but the man that used it most was the chief hunter; he could see things I could not. His eyes were used to the landscape, and at that time of the year the argalis were the same color as the gray stones. If they didn't move, I couldn't see them. And of course the argalis are very clever. When they have a suspicion that they are being looked at, they stand absolutely motionless—even for hours. They were generally in groups of about five or six males; we didn't see herds with females.

The argalis spend the night in caves or close to the mountainsides, coming out during the day to sun themselves and get warm. That is the reverse of what our red deer do, coming out only at early morning or dusk and spending the day under cover. For the most part we were hunting on a plateau—and this plateau is called by the Chinese "the roof of the world," because it's at 15,000 feet elevation. The surrounding peaks were perhaps 1,500 feet higher.

We spent many hours glassing the stony mountains and valleys looking for argali. My spotting scope was essential and my Leica binocular very helpful. So was my down-lined Gore-tex jacket, loden hunting pants, and Austrian woolen gaiters. Mongolia.

The Chill Factor and the Lack of Oxygen

At these temperatures, the wind was very, very cold. It was not so bad when one was moving on horseback or walking, but when one had to get down and glass for two or three hours, the cold really pinched. Sometimes we made the best of it and had a picnic lunch behind a big boulder for protection from the wind. When we sighted a group of rams it was necessary to climb above them to avoid their seeing us.

Walking was a problem among the slabs of stone—and because of the guide's pace, which, as in most of the world, was too fast. The difference here was that however much one had trained to get fit, the lack of oxygen caused one to tire, and there was no way of convincing the guide to slow down. He couldn't understand that coming from sea level affects one's stamina, and he seemed to take pleasure in demonstrating his superiority. As an additional torture the tips of my ankle boots were not hard enough, and as soon as I began walking and climbing among the slabs I bruised the big toes of both feet and had to bandage them to be able to move at all for the rest of the hunt.

A Good Argali and Our First Serious Failure

After about ten days, during one of those glassing sessions near the top of a mountain, we came very near to shooting a very good argali, the best I saw. There was a group of them on the side of the mountain opposite us, with a valley in between. They were moving downward. The chief hunter asked me, through the interpreter, if I could slide down behind him quickly, on my belly like a snake, because that was the best way to get down before they saw us: Like all sheep, the argalis have very good eyesight. The chief hunter thought I wouldn't be able to do it—but I did. It was really tough going all the way down. That's a very stony country.

The chief hunter offered to carry my rifle for me on the way down. That's standard practice with all guides, and in Africa they have gunbearers. The theory is that the hunter-

Riding up and down the stony mountain slopes above the clouds was not easy going, and sometimes we had to dismount and walk while leading our horses. Mongolia.

client should not tire, so that when it comes time to shoot he has a firm and stable hand. In this case, I don't think I could have done it with a gun over my shoulder. So we slid down. But when we got there, almost at the same time as the rams, they were about eight hundred yards away. We got as near as we could, but it was not near enough. When we saw them it was around 2:00 P.M. and they had bedded down for their siesta—with one of them always standing up as a sentinel.

At this point I should explain something that is important to what follows. The Mongols' society is primitive, and as in all primitive societies, hierarchy is very much respected. In my group, the head of the camp or the chief hunter was at the top. My interpreter was under him and always treated him with great respect. When we got down, the chief hunter decided that we should wait until near sundown, when the rams would get up and leave. He said they would do so at an angle returning on their tracks that would give me a good two hundred-yard shot.

I looked over the terrain and said to the interpreter, "Look, although this is the first time I've hunted argalis, my hunting experience tells me that they'll go off the other way. And if they do, I won't have a chance because the distance will be too long—about one thousand yards because they're starting from eight hundred yards away."

I asked him to explain this to the chief hunter and to suggest that, as we had quite a few hours until sundown, I could very slowly advance on my tummy and slither from boulder to boulder and get to a big one that was about four hundred yards from the rams.

I knew how my .300 Weatherby Magnum shot at that distance with my specially handloaded cartridges. I knew exactly how many inches they fell for a 400-yard shot. I had even demonstrated it on the way to camp in the Jeep and had had some cardboards put up as targets at three hundred and four hundred yards: I wanted to show the people in our hunting party that I could shoot at that distance so they would have confidence in me. But the chief hunter said no.

I said to the interpreter, "Please insist. This is a very good argali. We have not seen a better one, and I don't know if I'll get another chance like this."

But the chief hunter was adamant. He said, "No, no," and the interpreter told me we would have to wait.

"If he said no, it's no. I cannot insist further."

I was desperate, but there was nothing I could do. So I waited, and when the argalis got up near sundown, they ran off in exactly the direction I had predicted. I lost my shot.

The chief hunter said nothing. I was very mad at him, and now we were getting near the end of my hunt. The next day was a Sunday, and the chief hunter wanted to go off to the nearest village at 5:00 A.M. dressed up in his best clothes. But the assistant hunter, a much younger man, told the interpreter that he had an uncle whose tribe's pasturage was not far away and that he thought there was a group of good argalis there. He suggested we go, and we did—without the chief hunter.

Our base camp at an altitude of 12,000 feet had four big white round tents called yurts. Their sides were made of felt and sustained by long poles. Mongolia.

We drove off in the Jeep and got to the foot of the mountain in the afternoon. There was a group of argalis on the slopes, with some good specimens among them. We began to climb, but the light was already fading by the time we got near them. They soon went around the top of the mountain. We had climbed to 15,000 feet.

A Night in a Mongol's Camp

We lost sight of them, and it got dark. The assistant hunter said there was no point going back to camp, because it had taken four hours to get where we were and we would have to be back before dawn. The argalis, he said, would sleep there, and if we were early we could get close enough for a good shot.

"My uncle has his camp of yurts near here," the assistant said. "I'm sure he would very graciously accept you as his guest for the night." And he did.

I always say that the more primitive a people, the nicer they are. It's civilization that spoils man. I couldn't speak these people's language, but I could see that they were tremendously pleased to be my hosts. The whole family was inside the yurt—the mother and father, the children, the uncle, the aunt, the grandfather, and the grandmother. They all lived together. And they had all sorts of old cardboard attaché cases and bags that they used as closets, probably keeping their belongings in them.

The Mongolians' hospitality was first class. They invited us to dinner, but that, unfortunately, was a problem for me. The typical food of the Mongols is leg of lamb with very heavy fat—bad for my stomach, which has suffered a variety of problems over the years. They also eat the little onions that grow naturally on the land, and onions are something else that doesn't suit me. Both are bad for my stomach.

I had brought from Argentina small envelopes of dehydrated food containing soup, pasta, even chicken, as well as some biscuits and quince jam. I had carried a big canvas bag to Mongolia filled with this dried food, and when I got to the base camp on the first day I told the cook, who was the camp manager's wife, "I've just had an ulcer operation. I'm under doctor's orders. I have only half a stomach. Don't take offense, but I must have this to eat and nothing else." I told her how to cook dehydrated food in water, and she did very well.

But that evening I didn't have my food with me, so I ate as little as possible. We all sat in a circle, and the host passed a bowl round—they don't have plates, only bowls. The bowl of food was homage to the guest of honor, which was me. I had to return the gesture and offer him something, and the only thing I had to offer was my whiskey. By that time there was only about three-quarters of a bottle left. So I put a little bit of whiskey into the now empty bowl—not too much—and offered it to my host in return. He liked it. I had to repeat the procedure and offer whiskey to all the members of the family: a little bit of whiskey in a bowl to all of them.

The bowl went around with great success, and I had to refill it each time it came back to me—rather like a round of "mate" drinking in Argentina. We spoke through the interpreter, and it proved a very pleasant evening. I asked them about their life, and they told me how they lived as nomadic pastoralists. They considered themselves rich and happy with their sheep, goats, yaks, horses, and camels. They told me how long it took to graze an area, and how there was no authority to oversee or regulate them. They really did seem to live a wonderful life out there in the wild. They had everything: milk, meat, onions, and a lot of freedom.

When the dinner was finished I told my interpreter to thank them very much for their hospitality and tell them that we had to go because we had to be up at 4:00 A.M. to get back onto the mountain before the sun came up. I was just stretching out my hand to retrieve my whiskey bottle when, to my horror, the interpreter got to it first. It was still about half full of scotch whiskey, and he poured it all—every drop—into his bowl. There was a half liter left, and he gulped it down in an instant. He didn't drink it slowly, he gulped it.

My Interpreter Gets Drunk

When I saw what had happened, I thought that this is the end of my hunt. He'll be drunk as a lord, and what will we do? I suggested we go to bed. My party had one small tent that I used when fly camping. They themselves slept under the stars in their big cloaks. The tent was about twenty paces away, and as we were walking toward it the interpreter said, "Oh, I'm beginning to feel bad. Can I sleep in your tent?"

This was a tent for one. I said OK, but as we got to the tent he fell down like a log inside of it. He was out cold. I had great trouble in moving him to one side so that I could at least sleep alongside. I slept for four hours and awoke at 4:00 A.M. When I tried to awaken the interpreter he didn't move. First I touched him, then I pushed him, then I got hold of his hand. Then I shook him.

Nothing. In the end I shook him so forcefully that he did wake up. And when he woke up he was like a demon let loose. He woke up shouting, screaming.

"How dare you wake me when I'm sleeping! How dare you! I was sleeping peacefully and now you come and wake me up! I'm feeling rotten."

Of course he was feeling rotten. It takes more than four hours to sleep off a half-liter of whiskey. We went outside. The sky was still dark, and the men were not yet up. But they were sleeping outside and heard the fuss. There we were, in front of all the Mongols, and the two of us shouting—because if someone shouts at me I shout back even louder. I said to him, "You're a disgrace! You're an unfaithful interpreter. You're a bad official. When we get back to Ulan Bator I'm going to tell Zhuulchin what you've done, and I'll get you kicked out of the organization." This sort of thing went on for about ten minutes, with the men looking on.

I was worried that they might want to side with their fellow Mongol against me. After all, here I was, alone under the stars of Mongolia at 15,000 feet, surrounded by black, black darkness and all of these Mongols—with one of them shouting at me like a madman and me shouting back. I would have liked to have had a friend with me at that time. But I think that the men realized what was going on, and after a time the interpreter gave in a little. I don't know if it was what I said, or just my willingness to shout at him.

"Well, now," I said. "Go and have coffee immediately. We leave in ten minutes. We've already lost half an hour. You must get up and drink your coffee and off we go." And off we went.

We drove in the Jeep for about half an hour and then began our climb up to a little plateau. I looked at the interpreter as he got out. He turned to me and said, "Look, I'm feeling much better. Please excuse me. This has never before happened to me. Obviously I took too much alcohol. Please excuse me. I behaved very badly."

He was soon apparently sober, and I felt relieved. Apart from a headache, he seemed completely recovered. Fortunately I had my migraine pills with me, and one of them was all that it took to cure him—although if I hadn't had them with me, I might never have taken my argali.

My High Altai Argali

It was late when we finally got up near the top, and by then the argalis had gone around the mountain. The sun was up. It had been a steep climb, some 1,500 feet higher than where we had been before, and with the lack of oxygen my heart was thumping and my lungs seemed to want to come out through my throat. When we got around the mountain, the argalis had already started down the other side. But they had stopped on a sort of small plateau or ledge, and there they were, milling around. They were about two hundred yards straight below us.

Of course, they might be off at any moment. So we lay behind a boulder, looked over the edge carefully, and picked out a good one. I got onto my belly, and two of the men had to hold me by my ankles so I could shoot. It was straight down. Finally I got my body into position and placed the chosen ram in my cross hairs. Fortunately I hit it—and that was that: the end of an exhausting and bumpy hunt for a high Altai argali.

When we got back to camp we weighed the head, which came to fifty-five pounds. Mine wasn't a top trophy, but it was a representative trophy. The circumference at the base of its horns

Although I shot an Altai argali in Mongolia, I did not get a chance at a Siberian ibex. On another hunt, I shot this nice Spanish ibex that I hunted in the Beceite area near Barcelona. Although much smaller than the Mongolian ibex, it offers a very sporting hunt. Spain.

was twenty inches. It had thick horns, although their points were broomed off quite a bit because this was an old ram.

And then it was all over. My farewell words to the camp manager had been very dry, but at the airport I gave my interpreter a good tip. The only trouble had been when he got intoxicated. All the rest of the hunt he had done his best to get me up and around those mountains and to get everybody to support me. He'd done a good job—and I'd taken my high Altai argali.

Chapter 10

On Jaguars and Dictators

In between international safaris, whenever possible I hunted in my own country, Argentina, which is very rich in wildlife and trophy animals. Perhaps the most glamorous and prestigious of all Argentine trophies is the red deer, which always offers an exciting and demanding hunt. Red deer are found in the mountain lake region in the south, where long shots are the rule, and in the province of La Pampa, which is brush country and where shorter shots are usual. It is a very noble animal and considered a top trophy all over the world.

By international standards, however, I would say that there is one animal that is a top trophy not only in Argentina but also internationally, although nowadays it is protected. That is the jaguar, or *yaguareté*, as it is called in Argentina. The locals call it *tigre*—that is, tiger.

Jaguars and Leopards

The jaguar is similar to the African leopard, although it is heavier built and a little bigger. For example, its length is between six and more than eight feet, including the tail, which in the jaguar is a little shorter than in the leopard. The latter's body length, also including tail, is over six feet for big males. The shoulder height of the jaguar is about 30 inches, while for the leopard it is about 20 to 30 inches. As to their respective weights, the jaguar is normally between 200 and more than 220 pounds, whereas the leopard reaches only from 65 to a little over 150 pounds. Of course, the females are smaller in both species.

Naturally both have spots, called rosettes, on their bodies. The jaguar has larger and squarer rosettes than the leopard, whose rosettes are smaller and rounder. The color ranges from yellow to orange to a sort of orange-brown, according to habitat. I would say that the jaguar is probably of a deeper color than the leopard. Although they are both tree climbers, the leopard is a more agile animal, being lighter; it is known to leap more than eighteen feet horizontally and up to nine feet vertically. The danger of the wounded leopard is well known, springing from seemingly nowhere onto the unfortunate hunter. The jaguar also leaps, but not in the same way.

The leopard's habitat includes almost all of sub-Saharan Africa, including and especially forestland, but it can also be found in deserts, such as the Kalahari, where it is hunted by following its tracks. It is a nocturnal animal that is generally hunted by baiting, such as by hanging small animals like gazelles from trees and waiting at dusk in a machan or blind at a distance of fifty to one hundred yards.

Like the leopard, the jaguar can be baited. The tradition with the African leopard was that it be shot only in the last hours of the day or early hours of the morning, without using a flashlight, a tradition that nowadays is not respected everywhere. In the case of the jaguar, if it is baited and arrives in the middle of the night, a flashlight or artificial light of some kind is used. It is also common practice to call jaguar. That is not so usual with the leopard, although in some places, such as Central Africa, when they call in duikers they may get a leopard instead.

The jaguar is also hunted with dogs. That can make for a long and tiring hunt, and if there are rivers or wetlands in the area it will invariably get into them and make things more difficult—especially if it is during the rainy season. The dogs may have to follow, swimming, and the humans in a dugout canoe or on horseback. When dogs catch up with a jaguar, it usually climbs a tree and tries to remain out of reach. But sometimes it faces them on the ground, which can be very dangerous, both for the dogs and also for the hunters. The jaguar has powerful forelegs and claws, which it uses effectively. Nowadays in South Africa hunting leopards with a pack of dogs is becoming popular.

In the midnineteenth century in Argentina, there used to be jaguars right down the center of the country, in the plains area called the Pampean region. Because of pressure from man, loss of habitat, agricultural activities, and other such reasons, however, the jaguar gradually migrated north. Nowadays it is found only in the subtropical forest area, which runs from the Andean foothills in the northwestern provinces of Jujuy and Salta along a wide belt of the northern frontier to the most eastern of our provinces, Misiones, on the border of Brazil.

As happened with the leopard, the jaguar was put on the endangered species list, and hunting them was either forbidden or subject to conditions. In Africa, however, it has been proven that the leopard is much more numerous than had been thought, and I consider the same true in South America for

I hunted for jaguar with PH Juan C. Joy in a very thick and dry bushy area. One of the goats used as bait is seen behind us. Paraguay.

the jaguar. In many regions of Argentina there are farms within its habitat, and it is common for jaguar to attack and carry off young goats, sheep, and even cows—which they can easily carry away because of their tremendously strong neck muscles. This, of course, causes great animosity from farmers.

There is permanent discussion going on over the possibility of a regulated hunt with strict quotas. Such a hunt might benefit these cats, much as a similar one did leopards in Africa. The jaguar, by the way, was once the main sporting trophy in Brazil, but a few years ago all big-game hunting was forbidden there. Today there are more jaguars hunted and killed illegally than were ever hunted legally. As has been seen so many times, there is nothing that tends to the extinction of a species more quickly than a complete and absolute prohibition on hunting.

The Bolivian Jaguar

I had the good fortune in 1975 to be invited to join someone who was exploiting an important forest area in the north of Bolivia, and I traveled there for a short visit. It was really a ridiculously short period of time for a hunt, but that was all I had.

We spent two days and nights in a beautiful subtropical forest replete with all the animals typical of such a region, from wild boars to coatis to small rodents called pacas. We passed the first night on an elevated platform so as to lessen the chance that our scent would be perceived by the fauna, and during the day we explored our surroundings, which were very interesting and beautiful. We were able to shoot some wild boars that day. For our second and last evening a local expert in hunting jaguars was called in. This expert is known as a *tigrero*, and the name literally means a "tigerman."

The *tigrero*'s plan was that he and I would stand with our backs against a special tree, from which numerous fruit are dropped, attracting all sorts of small animals. As soon as it got dark, these small animals appeared, and with the aid of a flashlight I shot some of them. The *tigrero* told me that the

The main course for dinner in the subtropical forest was the very tasty white meat of the armadillo. Bolivia.

smell of their blood would attract a jaguar. After a while there were quite a number of them strewn about the tree at a distance of about ten to fifteen yards from where we were sitting.

Then we waited. Well past 11:00 P.M. I asked him what his plans were if a jaguar didn't turn up, because this was my last night. He said, "Don't you worry. In a little while I will begin to call, and he will come. You will see." The call, when it came, was a sort of mating call he produced by cupping his hands into the shape of a seashell. Some actually use big seashells for the purpose. With one thumb over his nose, he emitted a strong call.

About half an hour passed after he stopped calling. It was fall, and there were dry leaves on the ground. Suddenly I began to hear the stealthy footsteps of a cat. It was still a little way off, but one could not mistake them; gradually they came nearer and nearer, and my adrenaline began to pump. I asked my expert what was going to happen.

"Well," he said, "we let the *tigre* come right to us, because he is attracted by the smell of the small animals. When he gets to about fifteen yards from us, I will then put the flashlight on him, and you will see two green eyes. You will notice the difference, because all the other small animals have yellow eyes. The cat has two bright, deep, and profound green eyes that will look straight at you."

At that moment it was pitch dark, because the moon had gone down or was covered by the forest trees. The only thing you could hear were the footsteps, quietly approaching on the fallen leaves. I was dismayed to hear the *tigrero* say, "If I put the light on too soon it will run away, and you will not have a chance to shoot it. And, of course, I mustn't put it on too late, because then it will be too late for you to shoot it. His chance will be better than ours."

This was getting really exciting. My heart began pumping hard as I heard the steps approaching. On the one hand I was wishing that he would put the light on as soon as possible so the jaguar wouldn't jump on us, but on the other I didn't want him to do it too soon and let the jaguar get away. Finally and without any warning, he put the flashlight on, and there, sure enough, were two beady green eyes about ten yards from us. I didn't need anyone to tell me to shoot. I did so immediately, and the cat jumped into the air and sprang away.

Of course, shooting that way, I could only guess where the body was—whether to the right, the left, or straight behind the eyes. I started to run after the jaguar, but the *tigrero* caught hold of me and said, "No. You cannot run after it in this long undergrowth. It's much too dangerous. We have to stop. If you have hit it, it will be dead in the morning, not far from here and we will come back to get it."

The problem was that I had to leave early the next morning to catch a plane back to Buenos Aires, and I could not go and look for the jaguar myself. So I asked my host to please do that for me and let me know. To cut a long story short, a really disappointed hunter returned home, hoping against hope, however, that his jaguar would be found. But there are many scavengers in the forest that will tear up a fallen animal, and that is what happened.

A few days later my friend sent me news that my jaguar had been found only forty yards away from where I had shot it, but that during the night the animals of the forest had eaten it. They had had a big spree and, of course, spoiled its skin, so they couldn't send even that to me. Thus ended my first disappointing experience with jaguar hunting—although I had great fun facing a jaguar on the ground.

Paraguay

Sometime later, while I was minister of economy of Argentina, we had very active negotiations with the Paraguayans for various reasons, including the building of a big hydroelectric dam called Yaciretá on the Paraná River. The head of state of Paraguay at that time was General Stroessner, who had been president for more than twenty years and was not only the undisputed political leader of the country but also dispenser of favors and absolute ruler—rather like the owner of an *estancia*.

I had planned a visit to attempt to win over the goodwill of the Paraguayans by trying, as the stronger country, to concede most of what they were asking for—things of minor importance to Argentina that however meant a lot to Paraguay. My relations became very good with them as a result, and after the negotiations ended I was told that General Stroessner would be pleased to receive me officially in the presidential office.

My Meeting with President Stroessner

President Stroessner proved to be a charming man when I met with him, and he apparently had been informed that I had been helpful in the negotiations. As a result he seemed to take some sort of a liking to me. Our interview was successful, and afterward the head of the ceremonial department told me that the president had commented very favorably on my person.

The Yaciretá Dam was finally successfully financed, and after many difficulties an agreement was reached as to its

My first interview with President General Stroessner was cordial but difficult, because one had to guess the right opportunity to speak to avoid being interrupted by him. Asunción, Paraguay.

construction. Three years later the signing of the final agreement between Argentina and Paraguay was set to take place in the Palace of San José in Asunción, the capital of that country. President Stroessner, I had learned at this time, was himself a wildlife lover. As an example of his interest, there was an island that was going to be flooded once the dam was built, and he especially asked me to get our national park system to arrange that all the animals on the island be transferred to a natural reserve that he would establish in Paraguayan territory to keep them alive. He was also an avid fisherman who loved fishing for *dorado*, which is an outstanding game fish native to South America and found in the River Paraná.

At the termination of the negotiations there was a ceremony that was planned for which our president, the minister of foreign relations, a group of Argentine officials, and I were to travel to Asunción for the signing of the treaty. So off we went to the government palace of San José in Asunción. The ceremony was in the morning, and at midday there was to be a cocktail party held by President Stroessner in honor of the Argentine delegation. Prior to this one of Stroessner's top aides, with whom I had got to be good friends, had told me, "Look. Just a little secret. Don't let on. But when you go for the signing of the treaty, take a rifle and some hunting clothes." I didn't exactly know why, but I took them.

After signing the treaty, President Stroessner came up to me and said, "Minister, I want you to know how greatly I appreciate all that you have done to improve Argentine/ Paraguayan relations. I want to invite you to be my guest and hunt a *tigre*." Apparently he had been finding out from some of his aides what would be the best way to show his appreciation of my efforts. And that was how this hunt came to be.

"You will leave in an hour's time," he said. "My top aide will accompany you in my private plane with the commander of the army division from the area where the jaguars are. You will have the weekend—this evening, Friday, Saturday, and the morning of Sunday—in which to hunt and take a *tigre*." I was, of course, flabbergasted.

Hunting the Paraguayan Jaguar

When we took off in a small Cessna with the president's top officials, I looked out of the window and saw a DC3 that seemed to be escorting us. I asked, "What is that?"

"That's the presidential guard, his personal guard for you. They are accompanying us to provide for your safety, whatever you may need."

The flight took us straight to the town of Nueva Asunción, which is in the northwest of Paraguay, near the Bolivian frontier. From there we had to drive for two or three hours to get to the *estancia* of a friend of theirs, where we would spend the night.

To explain how I hunted my jaguar, I must tell the story from the beginning. It seems that when Stroessner was told that the best way of showing his appreciation would be to let me hunt a jaguar, he gave strict orders: "Arrange a hunt for the minister." At that time there was a very good professional hunter, an Argentine named Juan Carlos Joy, who was living in Paraguay. He took people out for, say, a fifteen-day hunt in

The taking of my jaguar resulted in a big celebration, both on the spot and back at the estancia. *The owner of the* estancia *is on the right of the picture and my friend Pilicho Remy Solá is on the left. Paraguay.*

the best area for jaguars. They spoke to him and asked him to organize a hunt for me.

Joy said, "I'm sorry, but it is impossible. I've already got a group of clients coming from abroad on that same date."

The top aide of President Stroessner replied, "Perhaps you didn't hear me rightly. I told you that the president has ordered you to take the Argentine minister to hunt a jaguar. That's it. Period."

The outfitter realized he had to comply. "But you can't expect me to get the minister a jaguar in two nights if I hold fifteen-day safaris to find them!"

"That's your problem. I'm only telling you what President Stroessner has said. Your business is to obey and comply with his orders."

What this outfitter did was quite clever. Normally, in Paraguay they put out live goats as baits. About five live goats were typically set out about thirty to fifty yards apart, and the next morning they are checked to see if at night the jaguar had killed any. Like the leopard, the jaguar won't immediately eat all the bait: It eats part and then covers it up a little and returns the next night. So this clever man, instead of putting out five goats, put out a string of fifteen or twenty to make sure that at least one would be hit. He set them out along the edge of the forest.

The first night I arrived a little late, and nothing much happened. At the ceremony I had met a friend of mine from Salta, Pedro (Pilicho) Remy Solá, the same person that had initiated me into hunting with a rifle, and I had been allowed to invite him to come with me. He sat at another blind farther along the road, and on the way back he was able to shoot a nice puma.

It's interesting to note how they set up their machans, or blinds. They are not like those in Africa, where the blind is built with leaves and trees, from fifty to one hundred yards from the leopard, with the bait up on the branch of a tree. Here the goat is on the ground some thirty to fifty yards from the edge of the forest, and that is where they build a blind—but not the kind you find in Africa. One is not supposed to

*The ring-tailed coatí (*Nasua nasua*) found in the subtropical forest is very agile at climbing trees, for it uses both its long beautiful tail and sharp claws. Bolivia.*

look through it. The hunter gets up only at the moment when he has to shoot, and then he looks over the top.

What they do is tie a string to a peg. The goat is tied to a peg, and the string goes straight to another peg that is in the machan at the hunter's feet. When one is sitting up for a jaguar that has already taken a goat on the previous night, one waits for it to begin eating. As it does it moves the goat, and the string breaks. What the hunter must do is keep his eyes glued to the peg. When the string breaks, it means that the jaguar is there. Then the hunter has to get up and shoot.

The next morning we went around and checked the baits and found that there had been two goats killed, one with very much bigger tracks around it than the other. So the professional hunter decided that this was the one we should wait up for, and he asked me to be there very early, at 4:30 P.M., to be able to get settled in before the jaguar came back. The *estancia* where I was staying was about a two-hour drive away; the jaguar baits were in the middle of some very scrubby dry bush, their special habitat.

When I got to the blind the PH was already there, and he told me, "Look, I have a feeling that this jaguar has not gone very far. I think he will be back early, so we must be very alert. He might be back even before it's completely dark." So we sat there for nearly two hours, and just as dusk was falling—it might have been about 6:15—a bird began to sing. The PH said, "You hear that bird? That's a sign that the jaguar is coming. Now be very alert." Not fifteen minutes later the string broke.

The PH looked at me, made a sign, and we both got up. There was still a little light, but the visibility was just awful. He put a flashlight onto the jaguar, and suddenly the scene was really very beautiful. The cat was a lovely color, orange-yellow, and when the light was on it looked up. I really would have preferred to have a camera in my hands at that moment. But I didn't. I lost what might have been a very beautiful picture. But one has only a few seconds for regrets once the light has been turned on. I put my Steyr Mannlicher .308—short, for use in forests, with a wooden stock and wood below the barrel right up to the muzzle—to my shoulder. I had some difficulty in finding the jaguar in the scope because I'd had no experience shooting in the dark with an artificial light. Then I fired, and the jaguar gave a big leap and ran away.

The PH said, "You missed."

I said, "No, I didn't miss. I put it perfectly well through the heart. Let's go see."

So we did. The jaguar was dead, ten yards from the bait. It had been the normal reaction to a heart shot.

Success and Celebrations

I felt a great elation, but I cannot describe the enormous relief the professional hunter showed. He immediately fired three shots into the air. The general and the top aide who had come with me were waiting about a mile away, and they drove up and began getting out bottles of champagne and whiskey.

I could see that they too were tremendously relieved, because they had had orders from President Stroessner that the Argentine minister must shoot a jaguar. We had a great celebration.

Back at the *estancia*, the owner greeted us at the gate in the traditional way—by firing off a machine gun into the air. That is the reception of honor. Inside, the celebration continued until sunrise.

That morning I had to get back to Asunción, and I didn't bother to change clothes. To my horror I found the whole Paraguayan cabinet formed on the platform at the Asunción airport to greet me. I had to shake hands with every one of them and receive their congratulations and the very special congratulations on the part of President Stroessner, transmitted to me by his top aide.

I was finally able to get on the plane back to Buenos Aires with my trophy. And that's how I took my first jaguar—or rather my second, if the Bolivian one that I never recovered is counted. I have never hunted jaguar again. The excitement and the thrill of those hunts had been enough.

Chapter 11

The African Leopard

The African leopard, one of the Big Five, is considered by many to be the most dangerous of them all when wounded. The leopard is one of the most agile of animals, both in the trees and when jumping on hunters searching for it in the long grass.

Going after a wounded leopard is one of the most dangerous things a professional hunter can do, and he will not normally let his client accompany him. Instead, he will take with him a couple of his men and a shotgun loaded with buckshot. A shotgun is the only weapon with which to face that amazingly quick attack from close quarters in the bush.

Countless injuries have resulted from tracking a wounded leopard, and if the cat gets its claws, which are full of rotten meat, into the hunter, infection will immediately follow. Today, with the availability of antibiotics, that is not as serious as in the past, but getting mauled by a leopard is extremely dangerous nevertheless. When a leopard springs upon a man, it tries to disembowel him by digging the claws of its hind feet into the victim's stomach.

A leopard weighs approximately from sixty to over one hundred fifty pounds. Its length is between six and eight feet, including the tail. The shoulder height is about twenty to thirty inches. Of course, I am referring here to the male, or tom; females are normally smaller.

Baiting in Leopard Country

The leopard is a nocturnal animal that is rarely seen in full daylight. Therefore it is one of the few animals that can be fully justifiably hunted at night with bait. For that purpose an antelope or gazelle is normally shot and its carcass hung over the branch of a tree after first being dragged over the ground to leave scent. The leopard never eats the entire bait in one night; it will come back two or three times depending on the size of the bait.

The hunters check the baits every morning, and when one is found on which a leopard has begun to eat, a machan is built—that is, a blind made of branches and leaves. This concealment is built at a distance of from fifty to one hundred yards downwind from the bait in a spot where the hunter can look into the sunset and see the leopard's silhouette against the sky. In some countries, such as Zimbabwe, they position the hunter so that the last rays of sun are at his back, illuminating the bait. When Tanzania was still Tanganyika, and a first-class hunting destination, it was forbidden to build artificial blinds for leopard.

It is also forbidden, although nowadays it's a rule that is not always obeyed, to use a flashlight on leopard. The hunter can shoot only when there is enough light. The leopard normally comes to eat the bait in the last light of the day, within the last half hour. And sometimes it comes when it's already dark.

Leopards are clever animals, and sometimes a week may go by with the leopard coming in each evening too late to be seen. Every day the baits must be checked in the morning and afternoon. If a leopard has been there, the hunter and his PH go into the machan and sit there from about 4:00 P.M. until sunset.

The Leopard on the Bait

When a leopard comes to the bait, it will jump up the tree noiselessly. One doesn't realize it's there until one sees it eating the bait. That's the moment to shoot—quickly but precisely, so it falls stone dead.

On my first safari, to Kenya, my son José and I spent a week sitting up for a leopard that was eating the bait but never came in early enough for there to be sufficient light to shoot.

Impala hindquarters are tied strongly to the limb of a tree for leopard bait, which is then covered with leaves to keep the vultures from seeing it. Notice the sky acts as a background so the hunter will be able to see the leopard on the bait in the last light of the day. Zimbabwe.

If we had done things the way they do in many places today, we'd have had a flashlight, waited up all night if necessary, and at the right moment put a light on the leopard. But that's not sporting. As a result, José never got his leopard. Poor *Toto!* (Swahili for *young boy*). I am hoping to get him back to Africa for another try.

The Leopard Hunt

After this experience in Kenya with leopard hunting, I decided to postpone my own leopard hunt, the last of the Big Four I needed, until I was able to take a safari in which I could have adequate time. That, of course, happens only when one has taken most of the plains game and other normally available animals and has the time to organize a specialized hunt. It occurred during my first safari to Zimbabwe, at which time there were only three trophies I was really interested in:

another elephant, a leopard, and a waterbuck, in that order. The latter I had never been able to take in my previous safaris.

The safari was organized through Ngamo as the outfitter, and I went with my former companion in Ethiopia, Héctor Pefaur, and another good hunting friend from Argentina, one who had not yet been to Africa. Our camp was on the majestic Zambezi River, in Unit 6 of the Matetsi area.

My PH was Neil Lindsay, a very good freelancer who had been called upon for me by Ngamo. Once I had taken my elephant, we began baiting in an area that Neil knew to contain good leopards. We were quite lucky, as after only a couple of days a seemingly big tom, to judge from its tracks, had fed on one of the baits during the night. A machan was immediately built about eighty yards downwind from the tree, opposite the direction from which the leopard had come from the forest. We didn't go back for it that same night; we wanted it to become confident on the bait and return the next day.

A Precise Shot

Previously, Neil had had me shooting at a target at the same distance as the one from the bait to the blind. He wanted to be sure that I could shoot straight. After I had proved myself, he next explained to me in detail exactly where on the leopard's body I should place my shot: at the top of the bottom third of the body, on the shoulder. If I placed it correctly, he assured me that the cat would fall like a log from the tree and remain stone dead at the foot of it. He added that, normally, after jumping up into a tree, a leopard would stand for a few seconds while trying to find a good position in which to feed. Then it would lie down on the branch and begin to feed. In lying down its internal organs would get compressed, and the exact position of the heart could be missed. Therefore he strongly recommended that I shoot while the leopard was standing.

A large part of the excitement and the nervous buildup for the leopard hunter is realizing that if he only wounds the leopard and it runs off into the bush, he will be responsible for the PH having to risk his life in going after it. There is no way to know, under those circumstances, if it has fallen dead fifty or one hundred yards from the tree, or if it is still alive and dangerous. A wounded leopard will jump on a hunter with no warning from such a short distance and with such a quick leap that it is very difficult to stop—even with a shotgun loaded with heavy pellets.

Darkness would fall around 7:00 P.M.; thus, we had a long wait, not moving or making the slightest sound. The boredom began to wear off, however, as sunset approached. About fifteen minutes before that time, I thought I heard a slight noise in the bush. I looked through the peephole in the machan, and to my

Comparing a .375-caliber cartridge with the leopard track was proof that the animal was a good size. Zimbabwe.

To show how large this leopard was, I compared my left hand with the leopard's paw. The sharp, retractable claws retain the remains of rotten meat, so a mauling by a leopard will cause a serious infection. Zimbabwe.

great surprise, there was the leopard on the ground, walking stealthily toward the tree, not five paces away. It suddenly turned its head, and its yellow eyes looked at me in such a penetrating way that our eyes seemed to lock. Its look was impressive and frightening, and so very stern that I had to believe it had seen my eyes through the peephole.

I grabbed Neil's knee to alert him, and after that small movement the leopard disappeared. Obviously, either the wind had changed and it had scented us, or, as my gut feeling told me, it had seen my eye. Neil was furious with me, saying that it was my fault the leopard had fled. I wasn't sure that I agreed, but there was no point in arguing.

The next morning we returned and put up a fresh bait; also, Neil decided to move the blind farther away from the tree because of the wind. We did not go back that night, but having checked the following morning that the leopard had been again on the bait, we returned to sit up that afternoon and evening. Neil had made me promise that I would not

I took this Soemmerring gazelle with a 400-yard shot. Danakil area, Ethiopia.

Glassing at high altitude for mountain nyala with PH Kidane. Ethiopia.

I took this mountain nyala with Nassos Roussos's Rift Valley Safaris. It ranks seventh in Rowland Ward's record book and sixteenth with Safari Club International. Ethiopia.

Héctor Pefaur, Nassos' charming wife Susan, and I pose with my 85-pound tusks at Nassos Roussos's Gura Farda camp. Ethiopia.

My lung shot struck this tusker as it was walking away from a water hole into the forest. Its tusks weighed 85 pounds each. Gura Farda area, Ethiopia.

At the Gura Farda elephant camp. From left to right: myself, PH Gabresi (standing), Rich Elliot, Nassos Roussos, and Héctor Pefaur with our tusks together with those of other clients taken earlier in the season. Ethiopia.

The buffalo fence, nearly 200 miles long, was originally built to separate the wild animals from the domestic cattle so they would not be affected by the tse-tse fly. Now that the area is free from the fly due to intensive spraying, the fence has reversed its purpose and is now protecting wildlife habitat from the intrusion of domestic animals. Okavango Delta, Botswana.

This Zambezi sitatunga is one of my most prized trophies, and taking it from a mokoro *in the Okavango Delta was a memorable hunt. Okavango Delta, Botswana.*

Walking knee-deep in the swamp toward an island in search of a sitatunga. Okavango Delta, Botswana.

I took this southern nyala in the southeast Malapati area not far from the Limpopo River. Zimbabwe.

PH Don Price and I admire my Chobe bushbuck, which ranks number ten in Rowland Ward's record book and sixteenth in Safari Club International's. Zimbabwe.

Pygmies and bongo in the tropical rain forest. Cameroon.

I hunted my crocodile in PH Don Price's concession. Zimbabwe.

The forest Pygmies are friendly people even though they look fierce with their front teeth traditionally filed to make them pointed. Cameroon.

Herd of savanna buffalo in a clearing in the forest. Their color is black and also a reddish-brown, similar to the dwarf forest buffalo. Central African Republic.

look through the peephole and not move until he signaled me that the leopard was on the tree.

It was getting very dark and I was just wondering if the leopard would not come when, at 6:50, I got the feeling that the leopard was there. Sure enough, Neil gave me the signal. The moment of truth had come. I slowly pushed the barrel of the .375 into the peephole and looked through the scope. It was dark, but there just enough light for my 1½–6X42 Zeiss on a 3X magnification to let me see the leopard against the sky. It was standing on the branch, moving around and trying to get into position to begin feeding.

I put my scope on its shoulder, and when it stood still for a moment I found the exact spot and squeezed the trigger. The leopard fell like a stone and lay still at the base of the tree. Neil told me to keep my rifle on it while he walked up to see if it was really dead. It was.

With an enormous sensation of relief I went up to the leopard, and Neil and I shook hands over it. I could not have felt happier. I had not put my PH at risk. Our Toyota soon came up with the boys of our team, and after the usual hand shaking and photos—taken with a flash because of the dark—we went back to camp.

My friend Héctor was also sitting up for a leopard, but his didn't come until the next evening. I was back in camp when all of a sudden Héctor and his PH drove up in a hurry and said that he had shot his leopard, but after falling from the tree the cat had bounded off into the bush. Héctor told me he was sure he had shot it through the heart.

I knew Héctor to be a very good shot, and I believed him—but of course nobody could be quite sure. Neil and I returned with them to the tree where the leopard had fallen, and both PHs went into the bush with shotguns to search for it. They did not allow us to go with them. Fortunately, about fifty yards into the bush the leopard lay dead. Obviously it had been a heart shot—although perhaps a little low, so that it had not cut off the top of the heart's blood supply.

We all felt very relieved, and that evening at camp there was a great party to celebrate the two leopards. All the hunting

Back at camp celebrating the success of the leopard hunt. From left to right: Héctor Pefaur, PH Neil Lindsay, myself, and Juan M. Romero Victorica. Zimbabwe.

and camp boys—including the cook, who was an expert dancer—began singing and dancing around the campfire in a sort of ritual leopard dance. Of course, abundant beer contributed to the gaiety.

It was a great night. At the end, all the camp boys and hunting teams came up one by one and shook hands with us.

We were blissfully happy.

Chapter 12

My Three Charges

I suppose it is the secret ambition of all hunters to be charged at least once by a dangerous animal—and to come through with flying colors. That, of course, is a fantasy in most cases, because one of the obligations of the professional hunter is to avoid having his client run into that sort of danger. After all, the PH is responsible for his client's life.

Over the course of my twenty-five years of hunting, however, I have had three charges, and they all ended happily—at least for me. I will relate them in the order in which they occurred, which is also the order of how dangerous they were, beginning with the least and ending with the most.

The Grizzly Bear

A group of friends from my fly fishing club organized a fishing trip to Alaska for silver salmon, and I was invited to go along. The fishing lasted only for one week, and as I had always wished to hunt in Alaska, I arranged to do it in the fifteen days following the end of the fishing trip. My main purpose was to hunt grizzly bear, Dall ram, and perhaps caribou.

Once the fishing was over, I flew from Anchorage to Fairbanks, which was where I would meet my professional hunter. On arrival he told me that we should hunt Dall ram first; this was September, and the season was about to end.

We began hunting in the Alaska Range mountains. It was impossible to travel there by Jeep or horseback, and even

My grizzly bear ranks number one in Rowland Ward's record book and fifteenth in the Safari Club International's. It charged me on the next to last day of my hunt. Toklat River area, Alaska Range.

walking was difficult because one sinks into the tundra. The standard procedure is to go out in a small plane, a two-seater Piper Cub, piloted by the professional hunter with the client in the backseat. Once the rams are spotted high up in the mountains, the hunter lands on the nearest dry riverbed. That can be a problem, however, because those riverbeds are strewn with big boulders; the pilot has to find at least fifty yards of clear landing ground on which to put down his plane. Once that is done the hunter and his guide go off in search of the animals, with the proviso that, by Alaskan game rules, they not be shot on the day of landing.

A Dall Ram

This trip was quite different from my previous hunting experiences. Once we had landed, the assistant PH and I had to put on backpacks containing the tent, a change of clothes, a sleeping bag, a little mat on which to sleep, and a small Coleman stove for cooking the dehydrated food. To get to where we had seen the rams we had to climb three ranges of mountains—that is, go up and down two ranges; the rams were at the top of the third. None of my previous hunting had ever required taking a heavy pack on my back. In fact, the sportsman-hunter was supposed to walk freely to avoid getting tired. Therefore I was completely unaccustomed to carrying a heavy pack—much less to climbing up and down steep mountains with it on. So I had a good excuse every now and then to stop and rest and look at the beautiful flocks of cranes migrating overhead.

It took us a full day of climbing to get close to where the Dall rams were, and there we spent the night. When we got up the next morning we found everything covered with snow. From that spot it was not a long climb to the rams, and

Hunting my Dall ram required a strenuous climb of three mountain ranges. It was on top of the third range with a small group of males. Alaska.

I finally took a good one with a two hundred-yard shot from my Belgian F.N. .300 Winchester Magnum.

Another interesting game rule to mention in reference to Alaska is the requirement that after shooting an animal one must butcher it and take all the available meat back in packsacks. That is because in Alaska there are no cattle, sheep, or goats to provide meat for the people. Therefore all game meat, excepting bear, is used as food. This requirement makes things much more difficult if one is high up and has to traverse two or three mountain ranges to get back to the camp.

Once at the bottom, near the dry riverbed where we had landed, we had to wait at our small camp until the PH came back for us with the Piper Cub. That did not happen immediately, and when he did arrive he said that he had seen a large caribou herd along the valley. This was the migration period, and in the middle of the herd he had been able to spot an extraordinarily good caribou bull, which he recommended I hunt. I really had no intention of hunting caribou, because of the time factor involved. But the PH insisted and said that if I did not hunt the caribou, he would. So I agreed.

Catching up with a Caribou

We left the camp side of the river and started off on foot to try to catch up with the caribou on the opposite side. That was a major operation, because the caribou, like the elands in Africa, walk very quickly and stop only once in a while to eat. We finally caught up with the herd, however, and the PH indicated which bull he had seen; it was an exceptionally good trophy. My first shot fell short, because the PH had estimated the distance at two hundred yards. I quickly corrected for a three hundred-yard shot, and fortunately the bull had not moved. It fell cleanly.

By the time we had taken the usual photos it was getting very dark, and then the skinning and butchering process began. At last we began the return trip to camp, which was a long walk in the dark. I had to shoulder the caribou's head, which was quite heavy and large, and the PH took all the rest of the

Catching up with a migrating caribou herd demanded a long and tiring walk in the tundra in order to take a good trophy bull. Alaska.

meat in bags on his shoulders. We got back to camp very late, and the next morning we loaded the little Piper Cub with all the meat and the trophy. The caribou head, however, did not fit inside the aircraft. The PH had to tie it under the wing of the plane, and I have a very interesting photo of us flying with our caribou head suspended beneath the airplane.

The problem, of course, was taking off with all that weight. Although the assistant hunter remained behind to be picked up later, it was a very heavy load, and we had only about fifty yards in which to take off before running into a boulder. Luckily, we made it.

Hunting the Grizzly

After having bagged these two animals, we were supposed to go up north to the Brooks Range, above the Arctic Circle, to hunt my grizzly. The reason was that there was snow there, and it would make tracking easier. Unfortunately we had a very inconvenient bout of bad weather lasting three days that grounded us. I spent those days seeing Fairbanks and especially visiting its natural history museum, which is really very good, with taxidermies of all the animals of the region. On the fourth day we again tried to fly to the Brooks Range but could not get through because of bad weather. As a result, the next day the PH decided that we should not waste any more time waiting for the Brooks Range to clear but should fly over the Alaska Range, which was nearer.

The grizzly is one of the most dangerous animals to hunt. It is not as big as the brown coastal bear of Alaska or the famous Kodiak Island bear, but it is much more agile, being

My guide, Fred Entsminger, and I are loaded with our backpacks as we commence the climb over the mountain ranges to hunt a Dall ram. Alaska.

swifter in its gait and quicker in its reactions. Its head and body length ranges from a little under 6 feet to about 8 feet. Its height at the shoulder is a little under to over three feet. Its weight is from over 440 to about 770 pounds. Of course, the males are bigger than the females.

One of the factors that make the grizzly so dangerous is its extraordinary capacity to absorb the punishment of heavy bullets. The animal has an enormous mass of muscle, and its torso is very strong and fleshy—which means that it is an animal that cannot be stopped by bullets hitting it just anywhere. The recommendation one gets about placing the first shot is that a bone must be broken to slow the grizzly's speed. One of the best bones is the shoulder, because the grizzly's normal gait is on four legs: It can run at a speed of about thirty miles per hour. Its eyesight isn't very good, but it has a tremendously well developed sense of smell.

To search for a grizzly we took off in the little Piper Cub and covered a very large area, ranging in elevation from the lowest to the highest—Mount McKinley, the highest mountain of the continent at over eighteen thousand feet and a very impressive sight. We kept on seeing animals, especially caribou, but there were no grizzlies. The land below was all snow and ice, rivers and forests. We started getting near to the end of my hunt, and I was getting worried.

The Toklat River Grizzly

Finally, on the next to the last day, while flying over the Toklat River, which is famous for its blond grizzlies—that is, bears of a much lighter cinnamon color than the normal brown—we saw one of a very acceptable size that was fishing for salmon in the small stream of running water left in an otherwise dry river. We overflew to get a better look and decided that, although it wasn't immense, it was sufficiently big to make a good trophy; anyway, this seemed to be our last chance. We flew off to find a place to land and then started our trek.

As we began walking, I noticed that my PH was not carrying a rifle. That fact had gone unnoticed when I was

The snow covered the sides of the small tent I shared with my guide the night before I took my Dall ram. Alaska Range, Alaska.

hunting nondangerous animals like the Dall ram and the caribou, but in the case of a grizzly one of the functions of the PH is to act as a backup with a heavy caliber in case of a charge. I myself had changed rifles and was now carrying my Browning .375 loaded with 300-grain Winchester Silver Tips. This .375 had already served me well in Africa, and I felt confident with it.

I asked the PH why he was not carrying a rifle as he should, and he told me that a few years earlier he had been out with a client had who refused to shoot a good grizzly, and, in a burst of temper, he had shot the bear himself. That had resulted in problems, and as a result he had decided that, inasmuch as he could not control his temper, he would never go out with a rifle again.

I wasn't at all pleased about the lack of backup, but there was nothing I could do about it now. I felt rather silly here in Alaska with only my own rifle—and my PH carrying nothing more than a penknife. Nevertheless, I was confident with my .375, and of course backup would not be necessary unless I were charged—and then I would be on my own.

We finally got to the area and camped, and the next day the PH went out to look for the grizzly. He soon came back to say it was still there: The grizzly was right in the middle of the river, still trying to catch salmon. But we had the wind against us, and so he said, "I'll go around and try to move the grizzly to get him to come up toward you, so you can get a shot at him." I was sure that would not be very easy, because our position was such that as soon as the bear became aware of a human it would run straight toward the forest opposite. I would then have to take a two hundred-yard running shot at it, which is something not generally recommended.

The Grizzly Charge

As I had expected, the grizzly took off running toward the forest opposite, and at its quickest pace—about thirty miles per hour. Resting my elbows on my knees, I took a swinging shot, estimating its speed as if I were shooting a duck. When the point of aim had reached perhaps half a yard in front of the grizzly I fired, and I must have led just right. There was a loud thump after I pulled the trigger, which told me I had hit its shoulder. The grizzly immediately stopped in its tracks, but it did not fall. It moved its head, sniffing the air, and as soon as it found my scent it came right for me. Of course, with a broken shoulder it was now traveling at half speed. I waited until it was about one hundred yards away and put a bullet into its spine, which anchored it. Only then did I put another into its heart. The grizzly finally fell to the ground and died.

My PH came running up to congratulate me, but I had rather mixed feelings. On the one hand I was somewhat resentful at his not carrying a rifle. On the other I was happy, inasmuch as everything had turned out successfully—and stopping the charge had been thrilling. But it is interesting to think that if I had missed either of the first two shots, the one at the shoulder or the spine, I would not have been able to stop the grizzly. It had enough steam up by then to run over the short distance that separated us, even with a heart shot in it. Although it would certainly have died from the heart shot, we would probably have died together embracing each other—rather a picturesque way of dying.

The Elephant Charge

Before recounting the elephant charge itself, I would like to set the scene by recalling my previous elephant hunts in Tanzania, Ethiopia, and Zimbabwe.

I took my first elephant in the Selous in Tanzania, with a side brain shot; the tusks weighed seventy pounds a side. A few years later I had a wonderful safari with Nassos Roussos in the Ethiopian forest at an altitude of about 4,500 feet. At that time Nassos had moved his elephant camp from Tepi to Gura Farda. We started off early every morning from an abandoned village where the elephants spent the night eating from the banana trees and then went off into the forest.

This was during the period when the Marxist dictatorship regime held the Ethiopian government, and in an effort to break up all opposition, army trucks fell upon the villages and

Nassos Roussos and Yohannis following the elephant tracks. Ethiopia.

Nassos Roussos's head hunter, Yohannis, is demonstrating the size of the tracks of the elephant I took. It measured twelve feet at the shoulder. Ethiopia.

separated the families that lived in them, relocating them elsewhere. This was a truly inhuman policy of separating families and ethnic or tribal groups.

From a hunting point of view, the abandoned village favored us as a starting point from which to follow the elephant tracks into the forest. After the second morning we were able to pick up the very large track of an obviously big bull elephant. For about a week we kept on following it all morning, until at midday it seemed to mix intentionally with the herd and we lost its tracks. Although big tracks certainly indicated a big body, they were no guarantee of heavy tusks—although they were more encouraging than small tracks would have been.

After an unsuccessful week had gone by, with a lot of walking uphill and down, Nassos decided that it was possible that the old bull would head for a water hole in the afternoon. Therefore we began methodically examining all

Although the tusks of the elephant that charged me had the lowest weight of the four I have taken, it is certainly the most memorable. Zimbabwe.

the water holes in the area. Finally, after several afternoons of following this strategy, we came upon one in a clearing just as a massive old elephant was leaving it, walking toward the nearby forest.

From the beginning I had told Nassos that I would not raise my rifle for anything under eighty pounds a side. That was my bottom limit, and he had agreed to respect it. As we got to the clearing Nassos immediately shouted, "Shoot! Shoot!" I raised my Rigby double .470 to my shoulder. The elephant was walking quite fast toward the edge of the forest, so it was not possible to try for a brain shot. I aimed fairly high at the heart and lung area and pulled the trigger from a distance of about forty yards. The elephant disappeared into the forest, and we ran in its direction.

Suddenly, forty paces from where the elephant had been when I fired, we found it stone dead, lying on its left side with frothy blood pouring from its mouth and trunk. Obviously, mine had been a very effective lung shot. After looking at the fallen elephant Nassos embraced me and exclaimed, "You've taken an 85-pounder! Congratulations!"

Zimbabwe Elephants

I hunted my next elephant in Zimbabwe. We had a very nice camp on the magnificent Zambezi River in Unit 6 of the Matetsi area, although we had some difficulties with Ngamo, the outfitting operator. We were a party of three, together with Héctor Pefaur and another friend who was an experienced hunter in Argentina but had never before been to Africa. The three trophies that interested me most were elephant, leopard, and waterbuck.

Every day we started our elephant hunt by driving along the road that bordered Botswana. In those days elephant hunting had not yet been reopened in that country, and as there was a severe drought at the time, the elephants crossed over to Zimbabwe; after feeding and watering, they went back across the border. It is well known that in Zimbabwe the ivory is much lighter and more fragile, probably because of the nature of the soil there; many of them had one of their

This elephant is not the one that charged me, but it came very near to doing so before turning away. Zimbabwe.

tusks broken off halfway, or nearly up to the lip. That made finding a good trophy bull all the more difficult.

Ngamo had assigned to me a very good freelance PH, Neil Lindsay, with whom we checked at close quarters the tusks of more than a hundred elephants. After many days of frustrating search we finally came upon a group of four bulls, and among them there was one that we judged was the best we had seen. As we were running out of time, I decided to take it, although one of the tusks was broken off halfway; it was, however, very thick.

We approached to about twenty yards, and I could have taken a side brain shot from there, as the elephant was standing quietly broadside in a group of four bulls. As Neil had not seen me shoot before, however, he asked me to take a heart shot instead. There was no time for discussion, so I decided to do as he wished. When I raised my Rigby .470 double, aiming for a high heart shot, there was a branch in my way, so I stooped a little, not realizing that a low heart shot would be the result.

Upon being hit the elephant took off at full speed, obviously wounded—but nobody, except myself, knew exactly where. We immediately followed the group with our trackers, and after one hundred yards, which is where it should have fallen from a high heart shot, one of them separated to the right in the direction of the Botswana border. I suggested we follow him, because my previous hunting experience told me that a wounded animal often tends to separate from the group. The trackers decided to follow the group instead, and we did so for the rest of the day with no success, because after a time we lost their tracks. My friend Héctor's hunting party came to help with the search, but with no results.

The following day we continued to look, fearing that the elephant might have crossed the border into Botswana, which would definitely have meant losing it. Neil decided on the third day that the only chance left was to look for vultures. We found them. At midmorning, driving along the border road with Botswana, we saw vultures in the air not far inland. We had run into my other friends' hunting vehicle, and we all jumped out and ran up the hill to the spot. On the

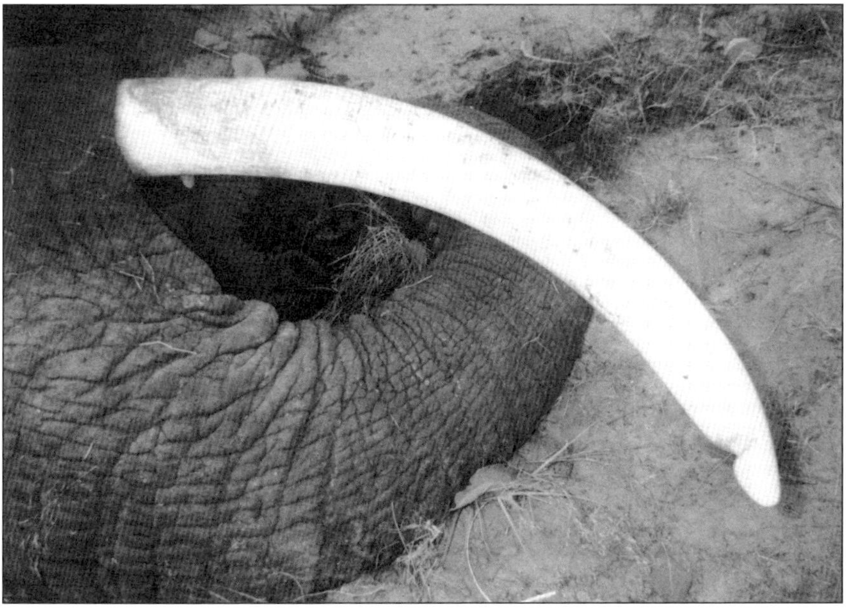

The left tusk has this small notch at the point for which I have not yet heard a convincing explanation. Zimbabwe.

approach we had to be careful, in case there was a lion or leopard feeding on the carcass.

When we reached it, sure enough there was my elephant—or what was left of it—with the vultures swarming over it, having picked their way inside the body. It lay exactly a thousand yards from where I had shot it, having broken away from the group in the direction of the Botswana border. This proved how far an elephant can run after being hit by a low heart shot, one that does not cut the top main vessels of the blood supply. As to its tusks, they were a little under 70 pounds—not up to the standards of my previous elephants, but the best that had been taken in the area that season. Afterward, I took my leopard and waterbuck.

Zimbabwe Again

After that we began studying with Héctor where we could find elephants with heavier ivory, and we were told that one of the best places was in the southeast of Zimbabwe, which is a kind of transit area where they come in from Mozambique and South Africa. There we would surely find very good elephants, as some 100-pounders had been taken in that region. We arranged this safari a year later and went off to a very good concession that Alan Davies had in the Malapati safari area, to the south of the Gonarezhou National Park. Unfortunately at the time we went we struck an extraordinarily dry period.

A Bad Drought

Because of the drought we encountered, there were not many animals to be seen. We walked our legs off and did manage to spot quite a few elephants, but none of them were what we wanted. We even went down to the Limpopo River, which is generally a big river with a lot of water, but it was almost dry, with only a little stream running down the middle.

Our fifteen-day safari was coming to an end, and we had not seen a good elephant. Again on the next to the last day,

The elephant charged, I made a frontal brain shot, and it fell ten paces from me. Its body was very big, and the speed at which it charged from twenty yards away was amazing. Zimbabwe.

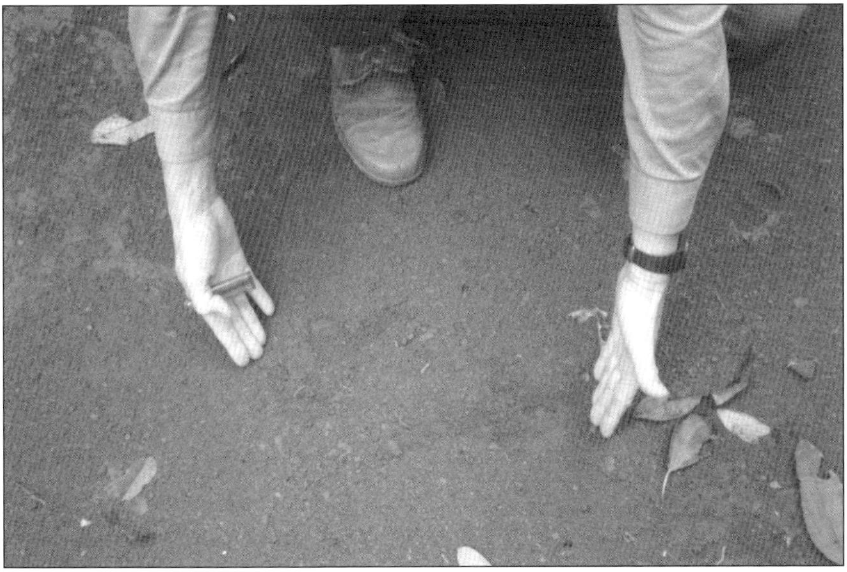

Walking along the edges of the tropical rain forest, we came across gorilla tracks. PH Alain Raoul is showing the size. Cameroon.

however, we discovered some very large tracks. Tracks were fairly easy to follow on the sandy soil, and since a large body might mean good tusks, we decided to follow. After several hours of walking we finally caught up and found the elephant tranquilly stripping the foliage from the trees. As we had the wind in our favor, it never noticed our approach.

We were able to approach to within about twenty yards. It was an old tusker, standing broadside to us, and in a whisper we discussed for about ten or fifteen minutes if its tusks were good enough. Alan Davies was trying to convince me that I should shoot, and at the bottom of my heart I wanted to, because it was the end of the safari and this would be my last chance. But I was not quite convinced. Anyway, at one point Alan said, "Move a bit to one side so you can get a better view of the tusks. Then decide."

The Charge

In spite of my moving ever so slowly, the elephant caught my movement. From its broadside position it turned suddenly around with an alarmed look on its face; although it had seen us, it must have been in a vague and imprecise way. An elephant's eyesight is quite poor. As it did not have our scent, it really didn't quite know what we were.

It glared at me for a moment, and then its eyes got red. I will always remember the redness of the eyes and the rage reflected in its face. Alan Davies, who had become a little separated from me, immediately said, "Shoot. He's going to charge."

I was still not quite convinced that I should shoot, and I very stupidly delayed following the advice of my PH. I had always thought that when an elephant began a charge it did so in a sort of ambling way, giving one some time. But we were only twenty yards away, and this elephant started to charge like a racehorse breaking from the gates. I cannot convey how impressed I was by the quickness with which it started that charge. It was all at once coming at me at more than thirty miles an hour from only twenty yards away.

I didn't need anybody to tell me to shoot now. I was carrying my Rigby double .470 express with the original 500-grain Kynoch full-metal-case bullets. I didn't feel hot or cold or nervous. I just automatically brought the gun up to my shoulder and immediately fired, as if I had been shooting a bird. I knew that the brain is somewhere above the eyes and on the level of the ear holes for a frontal shot.

And that was that. I thought, "This is happening to somebody else. It's not happening to me." As the elephant by that time was really quite near, the PH thought it was his obligation to back me up, and he fired at the same time. The result was that the animal fell with its tusks in the sandy soil ten paces from us. That was quite near enough for me.

When the elephant was down, Alan immediately told me, "Go and put a finishing shot into his brain in case he is only just knocked out." And I did, but it was stone dead. And that was it. It was over.

Our team of boys had stayed behind, of course, and they came up immediately after hearing the shots. Then the session of congratulations and photographs began. The elephant had fallen the way one does with a brain shot—or rather, two frontal brain shots. It fell on its side, not an especially good position for photography.

I immediately had the tail cut off. The personnel from a local crocodile farm were called in, and they skinned the elephant for us and took away the meat. I told them I wished to take all the usable elephant skin—the part that can be got from the middle of one side, around the belly, and up to the middle of the other. One can also take the ears, feet, and tail.

That is the story of the elephant charge. I can't say it wasn't exciting, but I felt very cool throughout. It all happened so quickly that there wasn't time to get nervous. It occurred to me that I had also been lucky, because this was my fourth elephant and I had taken them all with one shot, although differently placed: a side brain shot in the Selous, a lung shot in Ethiopia, and a heart and frontal brain shot in Zimbabwe. It was also satisfactory that all my elephants had been old bulls, which was proved not only by their bodies but also by the fact that their molars were very worn and they did not have another set pushing forward.

Leaving camp in the morning with PH Alain Raoul and his team of Pygmies to hunt bongo and dwarf forest buffalo. Cameroon.

By shooting them I had spared them a death by hunger, when they could no longer chew their food.

A Dwarf Buffalo in the Tropical Rain Forest

Of the three charges I had to face, the dwarf buffalo's was the most dangerous and frightening. In the case of a cape buffalo, one can generally see it coming from a distance, unless it is in very thick brush. But one doesn't see the dwarf forest buffalo until the very last minute, and that is the cause of the danger.

This charge happened during my safari to the Cameroon. The main object of it was to hunt the bongo, a very beautiful animal and one that is difficult to find.

The Tropical Rain Forest

The tropical rain forest of Cameroon, where the bongo, the dwarf forest buffalo, and dwarf elephant dwell, is one of the most difficult settings for a hunt. It is a thick forest with all sorts of intertwining vines and thorny branches that one has to get through. Going into this forest is like going into a sauna. One feels a burst of heat with a sort of stopping effect—then one gradually gets used to it. One's shirt immediately gets wet, both from the raindrops or the dew that falls from the leaves and from perspiration. The sun does not penetrate into this very dark rain forest, and there is no solar heat. On the contrary, although it is very oppressive because of the lack of air, it is really fresher inside the rain forest than outside under the burning tropical sun. This safari, both for bongo and dwarf buffalo, took place during the rainy season. It is at that time that the tracks or spoor can be followed.

The Pygmies

The Pygmies are the traditional inhabitants of these forests, and they are great experts, both in tracking and hunting. They live in small villages, building their huts with large forest leaves—very low and in the form of an oven or igloo. We visited the one nearest to our camp, where our trackers came from. They were very friendly people, with big smiles on their faces—especially if one gave them cigarettes. They greatly appreciate the safaris, because they profit from them. The outfitters also take care of their health problems and try to give their children some schooling. Off-season they go hunting monkeys, especially baboons, which are abundant, and other small animals such as duikers, using poisoned arrows and vine snares.

When hunting, one must follow them through the forest—and of course walking is impossible. One must crouch or crawl, because of the thickness of the vines and branches. The Pygmies move ahead, cutting a path with machetes or pangas; any movement would otherwise be impossible. The hunter follows.

The Dwarf Forest Buffalo

The dwarf forest buffalo is a relatively small animal. The Cape buffalo can weigh up to 2,200 pounds and has a shoulder height of more than five feet. The dwarf buffalo, on the other hand, weighs from 550 to 770 pounds and has a shoulder height of a little over three feet. That is, it is from one-quarter to about one-third the size of a Cape buffalo.

The dwarf forest buffalo has a brownish-reddish color—not the black of the Cape buffalo—and it has attractive fringes that hang from its ears. It does not have a boss but only two very pointed horns that slant dangerously forward. Like all forest animals, the dwarf forest buffalo is agile and aggressive. These forest animals are more aggressive than plains game, probably because of the nature of the enclosed surroundings in which they live.

One day, having found fairly recent buffalo tracks going into the forest, we left the vehicle and followed the Pygmies. Tracking can go on for hours, depending on how far the buffalo have penetrated, but with luck it might not be more than four or five hours. When the Pygmies realize that the quarry is near, they release small mongrel dogs that try to surround the buffalo and stop them so that the hunters can catch up. These dogs do not yap while running; their yapping begins only when they have surrounded the animal they are chasing.

To celebrate my elephant hunt, there was a special dance at camp. Nassos Roussos's hunting team carried me on their shoulders in spite of the rain. Young Jason Roussos can just be seen on the left. Ethiopia.

And then one has to go full speed ahead, trying to run through the thorny vines. Shirt, legs—everything gets scratched or torn by the thorns. The dogs can hold the buffalo for only a short time, and so it's head down with hat foremost to protect the eyes and drive straight forward to arrive as soon as possible.

We finally heard the yapping after about a five-hour crouching crawl and pushed forward to get as near as possible. But suddenly the yapping stopped, meaning that the buffalo had broken through the ring of dogs, which of course then returned to their masters, the Pygmies. When they did, the buffalo followed them. The dogs had provoked a charge by the buffalo.

The Dwarf Buffalo Charge

My French PH, Alain Raoul, had told me that there were probably five buffalo that we had been following, but three had separated off. Now there were only two. One had to look over the tops of the shrubs and short trees to find them, because the visibility below was limited to not more than five yards. Before long, we realized that there was only one buffalo coming toward us. We didn't know where it would come out of the forest, however, until suddenly at five yards' distance the forest opened like a theater curtain lifting and there in front of us, five paces away, was a stampeding buffalo. There was not much time for talk.

Fortunately I was carrying my double Rigby .470. I didn't even have time to bring it up to my shoulder to try to aim for the forehead; I had to shoot from the hip. It was a heart shot, penetrating from the front of the neck. Because the situation was so dangerous the PH also fired, from a position a bit more to the side. He had a .460 Francott. Although the buffalo had been coming straight at us, the impact of the two heavy 500-grain solids changed its course a little, and it passed us about half a yard to my side. Ten yards farther on it fell dead.

If it had not been for those two heavy bullets, put into its body at close range, that buffalo would have come straight at

With PH Alain Raoul and the dwarf forest buffalo that charged us. It has small pointed horns and fringes on its ears with no boss. Cameroon.

us and run over us or gored us, which is what generally happens in such situations. That is why I consider the buffalo charge to have been my most dangerous charge. If those two shots had not altered its course, I would not be here to tell the story.

Chapter 13

Spiral-Horned Antelope and Lost in the Savanna Forest

I have always admired the beauty and majesty of the spiral-horned antelope of Africa. Their evasive character, their well-developed senses of hearing, scent, and vision, and their agility make hunting them very sporting. The difficulties of the terrain in their natural habitat must also be taken into account.

All the spiral-horns display the qualities of beauty and majesty. Without putting them in order, I list the bongo, the mountain nyala and the smaller southern nyala, the greater and the lesser kudu, the sitatunga, the bushbuck, the common eland, and the giant or Lord Derby eland. All or most of them have one or more subspecies, especially the bushbuck, which has eight.

The Big Three

In addition to being hard to approach, spiral-horns offer a difficult hunt because there is a virtual absence of roads or trails creating access to their habitat. That obliges the hunter to go after them on foot, with long hours of tracking and searching, requiring a considerable amount of effort. It has been repeated many times that these trophies are not hunted, they are earned.

This very special group also demands that the hunter possess a superlative level of endurance, persistence, and obstinate determination. Some even add self-flagellation to the list. Also, as many times a trophy is not gained on the first hunt, numerous hunts are sometimes needed, which can give the whole business something of the feel of the search for the Holy Grail. The spiral-horned antelope that I call the Big Three are the mountain nyala, the bongo, and Lord Derby's or giant eland.

As to the similarities and differences between the Big Three, I shall mention them in general terms, because when dealing with each hunt they will come out in fuller detail. Both the mountain nyala and the bongo belong to the genus *Tragelaphus*, while the Lord Derby or giant eland is a *Taurotragus*. All of them have extremely well developed senses of scent, hearing, and vision, and all are difficult to find.

Their Habitats

Their habitats are very different. The mountain nyala lives mostly in the high mountain altitudes of Ethiopia, which is the only country where it is found, at over 15,000 feet. The climate up there is very cold, and visibility is poor because of an ever-present mist. There are frequent storms, and, because of the altitude, if at midday the sun comes out, it

Our base camp was at 12,000 feet, and I would leave on a small horse in the cold morning to get to the mountain nyala area. Ethiopia.

Kidane Biyadgo of Nassos Roussos's Rift Valley Safaris was my PH for mountain nyala. We spent many hours glassing the mountain slopes and valleys. Ethiopia.

burns human skin if one is not careful. The nights are extremely cold.

The bongo's habitat is exactly the opposite. It lives in the deep and dense tropical rain forest, at sea level of course. And it can be hunted only by finding its tracks and following them, guided by Pygmies, the real masters of the art. One must creep and crawl through vines and thorny branches. That, of course, is very tiring and exacting, and it can go on for hours and days until one finally catches up with a bongo.

Lord Derby's or the giant eland has in common with the bongo that one cannot see it, the way one can the mountain nyala: One has to follow its tracks. It does not live in a tropical forest like the bongo; its habitat is the forest savanna in a wide belt on the equator of western to central Africa. Dawn is very cold there, but things generally warm up as the sun rises. And if it is not cloudy, temperatures can get up to one hundred to one hundred twenty degrees Fahrenheit. Nights do not freshen up much until shortly before dawn, when it begins getting cold again. Giant eland are hunted by following their tracks, as you would with bongo, but their terrain is either open or forested savanna. One of the giant eland's characteristics is that, like all eland, they walk very fast for long distances without stopping. In the case of the giant eland, being much larger than the common eland, of course their steps are longer; if they get into a trot it is very difficult to catch up with them.

So the climates for the three animals described are different: extreme cold for a mountain nyala when it is hunted at those altitudes—although there are other, milder areas where they can be found around 4,500 feet. I hunted them up high. On the other extreme is the bongo, which to hunt one must withstand intense tropical heat and humidity. In the middle is the giant eland.

The Mountain Nyala

Taking a mountain nyala in Ethiopia, which is the only country in Africa where it exists, took me two safaris, both

PH Kidane and his hunting team surround my mountain nyala where it fell in the heather. Ethiopia.

After taking my mountain nyala, I found that hunting klipspringer in the mountains was very sporting. Ethiopia.

with the same companion, Héctor Pefaur. In the first trip, we were going to end our safari hunting elephants. The elephant I took in Ethiopia was a good one, an 85-pounder. But before going to the elephant area I went to hunt mountain nyala. For my friend, who had hunted less than I and therefore needed a more general bag of game, I suggested the Omo Valley, a beautiful area in Ethiopia, where he could hunt all sorts of plains game and important trophies such as the Nile buffalo, the Abyssinian greater kudu, the lesser kudu, the Grant gazelle, and some others. He took my advice and did very well.

Meanwhile, it took me more than twelve hours in a hunting car to drive from Addis Ababa to the area of the Arusi Mountains, where we were going to hunt atop Mount Badda. On the way we enjoyed watching the local form of public transport—minivans crammed with people . . . and with goats on the top. It was all very picturesque, and the people were friendly.

When we arrived at the foot of Mount Badda, a group of inhabitants came up to us from the village. The children, as usual, asked for sweets—this time in Italian: "*Caramela! Caramela!* Please, *caramela!*" Fortunately, we had brought some. The three big influences that the Italians had left behind in Ethiopia were pasta, pizza, and the word *ciao* for good-bye. We also say *ciao* in Argentina, and it was odd for me to hear it here.

This little village at the foot of Mount Badda provided us with the men and some small and shaggy horses that were to assist us in our hunt. By the time we got to the camp at the top of the mountain, it was almost dark. By then it was very cold, and the camp's installations were rather primitive. I was given a tent with a coal stove. The tent was not in great shape, though, and the coal was scarce. I was told that this kind of weather was normal, and that although this was the end of February, the weather would be one of our main adversaries.

The next morning we were up early. To get to where the mountain nyala were expected to be took a walk of about two hours. We were on top of the mountain, where the terrain was stony and difficult. The hunters were provided with ponies or little horses to get us to the hunting area. Although I consider myself an accomplished horseman, riding these little

It often rained for a short while on our way from base camp to the mountain nyala hunting area. Here the whole party is huddled under the protection of rocks. I didn't have an umbrella, but my waterproof camo poncho was good enough. Ethiopia.

horses was not easy. To begin with, they had a sort of wooden saddle, with high pommels both in front and behind, that made it difficult to swing one's leg over when getting on and off. Also the girth was loose and couldn't be tightened because the horse would then throw itself on the ground. Once on the saddle, riding was a sort of balancing act, going up and down the hillsides sideways. In addition, one got onto the horse from the right-hand side, which I have never seen done anywhere else in the world.

Our hunting party was quite large, and as the local people are very poor they all wanted a job. We ended up with a sort of procession in which every local man or boy carried something, even if it was not too heavy. The extraordinary thing was that, because it rained every half-hour or so, they all carried umbrellas. My rifle, in a very good padded case, was carried by one of the locals on whom I kept a relentless eye. I didn't want him bumping it, because of the delicate telescopic sight, an 8X56 Zeiss.

The Hunting Area

When we got to the area where the nyalas supposedly were, I got down from my horse and so did my PH Kidane, one of Nassos Roussos's professional hunters. And then we began walking along the edge of what were big valleys. We had to keep glassing down the slopes into the valley and up the next ridge of mountains to try to see nyalas. There are two difficulties in seeing these animals. The first is the weather. Because of the storms, the low clouds, and the mist, these large valleys are obscured until about midday. When the mist lifts, one can then see the heather in the valleys and on the slopes. Heather is a large, high shrub, and when a mountain nyala is bedded or lies down it is completely hidden. One can spot it only when it gets up.

Unlike our red stags in Argentina, which are out during the early and late hours of the day, when the nyala come into the open to graze, they have absolutely no timetable. One might see them or not at any time of the day. So glassing is the only way to find them. Fortunately I had taken my spotting scope with me. The nyala is a big animal, but distances are great, and it may be far away or hidden by the vegetation. So one spends every clear moment of the day, when there are no clouds or mists, glassing the valleys and the slopes of the mountains, walking along, glassing and glassing and glassing. My Leica 10X50 binocular was also of great help.

This went on for fifteen days, and in all that time I never saw a mountain nyala, either male or female. We even stayed out fly camping so as not to lose two hours going back and forth from the main camp. But it was of no use, and in the end, on one very stormy night, our fly camp got flooded out. That was the end of it.

Fortunately the second part of the hunt was good. That was when I rejoined my friend, who had been very successful at the Omo Valley. We went together to the elephant forest area, where we were able to take very good elephants, this time guided by Nassos Roussos himself, who is a great specialist on elephants. Thus ended our twenty-eight-day safari, with a brief stopover at a lower forest area for a Menelik bushbuck and a quick trip to the Danakil plains to take a Soemmerring gazelle, both of them Ethiopian specialties.

After my first safari to Ethiopia, the obsession for taking a mountain nyala remained with me. But it took me four years to get back. At one point elephant hunting was closed, but when it reopened my friend and I decided on a combined hunt for elephant and mountain nyala. Nassos Roussos's representative in the United States, Rich Elliott, told us that to avoid the bad weather we should leave a month earlier—that is, at the end of February—and have a twenty-eight-day hunt for elephant and nyala lasting till the end of March.

We were all prepared for that when suddenly at the beginning of January we got news from Rich Elliott that elephant hunting had again been closed. The Ethiopian government had accepted a donation by a European Community organization that they could use to build tourism on the condition that they forbade elephant hunting. That

With PH Kidane and an eastern bush duiker, which was fun to hunt as it was very quick and agile. Ethiopia.

was a great disappointment, and my friend Héctor Pefaur decided not to go. I couldn't bear the thought of not trying again for a mountain nyala, however. So finally I convinced him to come along with me, and off we went.

Perhaps to compensate for the bad luck of my first hunt, I was very fortunate in that on the sixth day, as we were walking along one of the high ridges above the mist-filled valley, we arrived at a good vantage point where we decided to stop and have a picnic lunch. While we were there the mist suddenly lifted, and looking across the valley to the opposite slope we saw a very good mountain nyala with two females. They were directly in front of us on the other side of the valley but completely out of range. We couldn't move straight forward, because they would see us and escape. So we had to go all the way around, in a big circle, and try to get across to the other side and onto the top of the opposite mountain. Then we would have to slither down on our bellies through the heather that grew on the slopes until we got within shooting range.

This procedure took a great effort and about four hours. We left at around 2:00 P.M. and arrived at 6:00, with not quite an hour left until sundown. By then the nyala had moved a little farther away and up the opposite slope, in the direction from which we had come. We slithered down through the heather until we got to where the heather line ended. Then there was no more cover—the valley was covered in grass. The nyala was now grazing quietly, broadside to us, although it had moved a bit higher up. Looking through my scope, I decided that it was just a little under five hundred yards off. Without saying anything, I asked my PH, what he thought the range was. He said exactly five hundred yards.

A Very Long Shot

I was flabbergasted, because I had been prepared at most for a four hundred-yard shot. I had a special handloaded cartridge with which I had practiced at home very thoroughly. I had taken my .300 Weatherby Magnum with me. It was the new model, the Euromark, which can take a longer cartridge than the former one, and so my cartridges had very good ballistic performance with a 190-grain S.P. Interlock Hornady bullet. But I had tried it only up to four hundred yards, at which distance I was sure of its trajectory. I was very doubtful whether I could shoot at five hundred yards with precision.

My PH said, "Look, this is your second time here. We have only half an hour before sundown. If we wait for tomorrow we may not see him again. You might as well take the chance, if you can get yourself in a comfortable position."

Fortunately I had taken a bipod with me, so I sat down, leaned my back on the mountainside, and steadied the rifle. I made a quick estimate of what the trajectory of the bullet would be at five hundred yards and aimed at the level of the top of the head. My PH gave me a very good piece of advice: "Don't try to hit the shoulder or heart, but aim to break his hindquarters. That will paralyze him and he won't be able to get away. If he's wounded and moves, we will lose him in the heather and never find him."

So I aimed high, but on top of the hindquarters. Well, God was with me that day, and I was very, very lucky. I held my breath and slowly squeezed the trigger. I couldn't believe my eyes when I saw the nyala fall with its legs upward, kicking in the air. Obviously, it couldn't stand up. So we ran up to it—it seemed such a long way across that valley full of stones and vegetation—and I placed a finishing shot. The first bullet had completely destroyed the right hindquarter, messed up all the animal's insides, and exited through the left hindquarter, leaving a neat little hole.

It was an old bull with horns over 37 inches long around the curve—a very good trophy. I couldn't believe my luck.

The next day we broke camp. I got on my little horse, and the whole procession began walking back toward the main camp. As we got near, the whole party began chanting a sort of victory song. The victory song is special and different for every region and animal. It was a grand moment, walking the last mile into camp with all the group singing and the people rushing out with their congratulations. This had happened to me on my previous safari to Ethiopia, when I had taken that very good elephant.

One of the sad things was that Héctor Pefaur never saw a mountain nyala during the whole fifteen days. Once I had taken mine I lent him my PH, who was perhaps more experienced than his, and I remained with some assistants at camp. I also lent Héctor my rifle, as I had a spare and his had been bumped on the scope by a bearer. While awaiting his return, I shot some small animals like klipspringer and eastern bush duiker, which were typical of the area. They were great fun to hunt, as they are quick and agile.

The Bongo: A Safari to Cameroon

Three years after taking the mountain nyala, I was able to organize a safari to Cameroon, which according to the advice I had received had some of the best bongo areas. On this bongo hunt, I had convinced my friends Héctor Pefaur, who had hunted elephant with me, and Ricardo

Chiantore, my predecessor as president of the Argentina chapter of the Safari Club International, to come along and hunt bongo with me. We arranged our safari through Gilbert Tarriere of 3W International, who got us very good PHs: Alain Raoul and his team.

After landing from Paris in the capital of Cameroon, Douala, we took a small plane to the Kika area, where our base was an abandoned logging camp. I hunted with Alain, my two friends with one of his associates. Most people go bongo hunting with a .375 caliber rifle and a telescopic sight that can be brought down to one or two magnifications. Knowing, however, that it would be a very close shot and that a heavy bullet would penetrate the thick foliage and branches more easily, I had decided to take my Rigby .470 double express with 500-grain Kynoch cartridges and, of course, open sights. It turned out to be a good choice.

The bongo is a magnificent animal. It is majestic and beautiful, with wonderful lyre-shaped horns, a lovely expression on its face, and the white chevron and typical white stripes that go down its side. Its color is a light chestnut like that of a horse—a little reddish.

The bongo has always been considered one of the most elusive of animals, and hunters have tried again and again to take them without success. In the Sudan, when hunting was at its height, the bongos were exceptionally good in the forest on the western bank of the Nile. Before that, the so-called eastern bongo was one of the top trophies of Kenya during its heyday, in the relatively small area of the Aberdare Mountains. In one of the most difficult of terrains, the bongo became famous because of the many hunters who tried unsuccessfully to take one.

When Kenya closed down hunting, the next area for bongo was, of course, Sudan. And when that country was out for all hunting purposes, the Central African Empire and later Cameroon became the main destinations for bongo. The western bongo, which is found mainly in Occidental African countries, is virtually the same as the eastern bongo of Kenya, although perhaps a little lighter in coloration. But it can be found over a larger area, though always a difficult quarry because of its elusive character and the way it has to be hunted in thick forest.

Hunting the Bongo

There are various ways of hunting the bongo. Walking through the forest is one: trying to find their tracks, cut the spoor, and then follow. The other is to build a machan or blind at the edge of a salt lick or some water hole that the bongo may approach to drink. That is the less sporty way, although perhaps inevitable for some people who cannot face the stress of walking enormous distances through the forests. Approaching the bongo is very difficult, because it has a tremendously acute sense of hearing. And too, the hunter might be able to see only a patch of reddish-brown skin amid the thick foliage. Many times he might not see the head or horns, and therefore might not be able to distinguish if it is a male or female, or its age. The

Pygmy village with their oven-shaped huts made of big leaves from trees in the tropical rain forest. Cameroon.

females also have horns, although they are shorter; in most countries if a hunter shoots a female he is penalized by having to pay double the price of a male.

All of this has made the bongo one of the most famous of international trophies. And even in the heyday of the Central African Empire, it was still a very difficult animal to obtain. A little later Cameroon came into being, considered a good destination for hunting bongo. There were enormously large and old forests there, in which logging operations were undertaken. Narrow trails, wide enough for a vehicle to go through, were opened, and that made a big difference to hunters. During the rainy season hunters go along the various trails that fan out into the forest to find bongo tracks. The animals move by night, and if the tracks are fresh the hunter has to follow them immediately.

The tropical rain forest in which the bongo lives is thick, deep, hot, and humid. It is very difficult to make one's way through it—it's a question of virtually crawling on hands and knees through clinging vines and thorny branches. On going in, the hunter can have no idea how long it is going to take to catch up with a bongo. He must be prepared for a long and tiring pursuit. Finding one may take hours or days.

The Pygmies

The secret of bongo hunting in Cameroon lies with the Pygmies. They live in quaint little villages in small huts like igloos or ovens: round huts, the sides and roof of which are covered with the wide leaves of the forest. Of course these dwellings, being as low as they are, would not be suitable for a man of normal height. But they are perfect for the Pygmies.

When we visited one of these villages we found all of the inhabitants very friendly. They are good humored, and, of course, the outfitters take care of them when they need medical assistance or other sorts of help. From these villages come the members of the Pygmy team who make the difference between the success or failure of a hunt. Pygmies have an enormous expertise in following tracks in the forest. In the rainy season there are many leaves on the ground, and the tracks are not only on soil but also on leaves; every little detail gives them a clue as to where the animals are going—things, for example, like broken branches.

When one follows Pygmies into the forest, the first feeling one has is the shock of temperature and humidity; it's like going into a sauna, although after a while one recovers. There is no stopping—it's all crawling or crouching. One's shirt is immediately drenched from the water of the dew or rain that falls from the trees.

When the Pygmies see by the tracks that the quarry is near, they release two or three little dogs, just as they do when hunting buffalo. These dogs run along following the tracks but do not yap until they catch up with and surround the bongo. Then they begin their yapping. When one hears this yapping one has to start to run immediately—run right through

Pygmy calling in a duiker by holding his nose and emitting a wailing sound like that of a wounded animal. Occasionally this technique brings in a leopard, which is always a surprise to the hunters. Cameroon.

vines, thorns, branches, anything, to get there as soon as possible. The bongo will be fighting the circling dogs with his horns and trying to break through.

The use of dogs by the Pygmies has been controversial, inasmuch as it was not done here in the past. Some people consider it unsporting. In my experience, however, what the use of dogs gives the hunter is an opportunity, a very short opportunity, to see his quarry and not to have to shoot through the foliage at a patch of brown skin. He can see if it's a female or an immature animal—and if that's the case not shoot. Most shots are taken from a distance of from ten to twenty yards, and then one must be very careful not to hit a dog. The Pygmies—and the French outfitters—value those animals more perhaps than human life: They are very difficult to replace and are essential for hunting.

My Bongo Hunt

On the day I took my bongo, we had been walking and crawling for three or four hours before the dogs began yapping. In my hurry to get through the vines and branches, my eyeglasses were ripped off my face, and I lost some minutes in going back to pick them up. But that was long enough for the bongo to break through the encircling dogs. When that happens, the dogs stop yapping, and as a result we thought the bongo had escaped. After a few moments, however, we realized by the movement of branches in the thick forest that it was coming our way. True visibility in this forest is limited to no more than five yards.

The whole party stood there expectantly. Then all of a sudden, only five yards away appeared the majestic bongo in all its beauty, running fast but not charging. It was merely running away from the dogs, and we happened to be in its way.

It was coming more or less straight at us, and fast. I was just able to sidestep and raise my double to my hip. There was no time to get it to my shoulder. The bongo ran past on my left side only a few yards off, and I got a running shot and hit it in the shoulder. It didn't fall, though, because its impetus was too great, and because it ran on, everyone but one Pygmy, and even the PH, thought I had missed. In fact, the PH scolded me for shooting offhandedly that way. He said, "You know, you might have shot a man or . . ." He didn't say it, but he meant that I might even have shot a dog.

I answered, "No, I knew perfectly well where I was shooting." I had been on the outside edge of the group, and there was nothing in front of me but that bongo. I had waited for it to come alongside, two or three yards away, and swung my rifle around. The bullet hit the animal just a little too far forward. The shot didn't hit the heart, but the bullet entered the shoulder just in front of the heart. The impact of a .470 caliber with a 500-grain bullet at that distance, however, is significant. The bongo didn't go far before dropping.

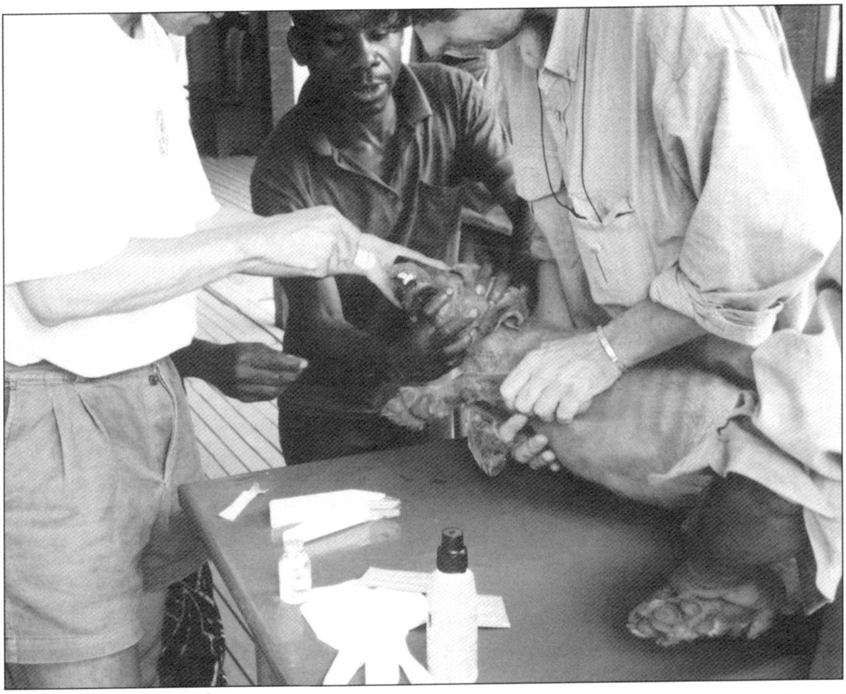

The Pygmies' dogs often get hurt when they surround a bongo or a dwarf forest buffalo, and their wounds are closed with a suture placed by a hand clip machine. Cameroon.

I took this majestic bongo in the tropical rain forest, thanks to a quick shot with my .470 Rigby double express rifle. Cameroon.

Of course the dogs had followed, and they immediately surrounded it. I quickly ran up and put in a finishing shot, always taking care of the circling dogs. What made it difficult was that the bongo was in the shade. The whole context was very dark, and visibility was poor. But I could not delay too long, because the PH was fearful of the bongo's hurting or even killing one of his dogs with its horns. So I wasted no time. And that was how I took my bongo.

After the photographic session, which went on for quite a time, we had the problem, of course, of evacuating it from the forest and walking back. That the Pygmies did easily, however. They cut big leaves from forest trees and used bamboos for stretchers or cradles in which they put the meat. The trophy head was carefully hung from the back of one of the Pygmies with a strong vine holding it firmly across his forehead.

Once back at the vehicle, we made our way to camp. And as we got nearer, the Pygmies broke out chanting their triumphal song. I felt rather like Caesar with his legions marching victoriously into Rome.

The Lord Derby or Giant Eland

Nearly two years after my successful bongo hunt, at the beginning of February, I flew straight from the Safari Club International's Convention in Reno to Paris. I was president of the Argentina chapter at the time, and I had convinced three other members to come with me to Central Africa to hunt giant eland. One was my old friend from Salta, Pedro (Pilicho) Remy Solá, who had initiated me in hunting with a rifle. Another was Eduardo Gerlero, an avid hunter who was vice president of our SCI chapter. The third was José (Pepe) de San Martín, who a few years later was to become my successor as president of the Argentina chapter of SCI.

Off to the Central African Republic

France still maintains strong relations with her former colonies, and once I had visited them I realized, both in Cameroon and in Central African Republic., that almost everybody speaks some level of French. Not only some Pygmies in Cameroon but also the local boys that formed our team in the Central African Republic all spoke French, some quite well and others well enough to make themselves understood.

When we landed in Bangui the outfitters' representatives were there waiting, and having passed customs we got on a charter plane that was to take us to the central camp of a hunting area measuring 770,000 square miles and covering all sorts of regions and climates. The camp, we soon discovered, had very nice rondavel huts with thatched roofs, with a good bar and mess that had a dining room with open sides and thatched roof. There were good beds, and the washbasin and shower were under the same roof; the toilet was outside in a different hut. Altogether it was a very pleasant camp.

We divided up according to what animals we wanted to take. Eduardo Gerlero and I were after the giant eland as a primary trophy, and Remy Solá and de San Martín wanted a leopard, followed by other minor animals. Eduardo Gerlero and I had to go farther inland in different directions to hunt our elands. We left the next morning in four-wheel-drive Toyota hunting cars, and it took about a day to get to our camp, which was very similar to the central one but smaller.

Hunting the Giant Eland

We arose on the first day of the hunt at around 4:00 A.M., because we had a two-hour drive to get to the area where the elands were supposed to be. It was very cold. At that hour one had to keep warm with a good jacket. About 6:00 or 6:30, just at dawn, we arrived at the place where we hoped to pick up the tracks. Giant eland in this region generally spent the night in salt licks and then, at dawn, returned to the forest. That was the moment when one had to cut their spoor to be able to follow them.

Here we are with a red-flanked duiker I took in the savanna forest. Bush duikers are not called in like the forest duikers in Cameroon. Central African Republic.

This evening dance at camp celebrates my return after taking a giant eland and being lost in the savanna forest. The camp members tied empty Coca-Cola cans with stones inside them to their knees, which sounded like a tin band. Central African Republic.

The equatorial forest-savanna here was not tropical, as in Cameroon, and some parts were open; others were quite dense. The trees of the forest had rather thin trunks that allowed one to see through them in the autumn and winter months, but visibility declined with the arrival of the spring leaves. Now, in the middle of February, winter was coming to an end, and most of the leaves were still on the ground. But although that had the advantage of giving a clearer view, it also was a disadvantage because they were noisy to walk on. Eland have sharp hearing, and thus the approach to them was always difficult.

The giant eland, unlike the bongo and the mountain nyala, is normally found in large herds—with the exception of some old bulls that become solitary. Every morning we found tracks and followed them, sometimes all day, but they were not very fresh. For the first six or seven days we never caught up with a herd.

The enormous size of the animal is impressive. Its height is around six feet at the shoulder, and its weight is about a metric ton. With its long stride and the fact that it doesn't

Caught in a tropical rain shower, which didn't last long, on our way to hunt giant eland. Central African Republic.

stop walking even when browsing, the animal demands physical exertion from the hunter lasting hours and sometimes days before one can get up close. That chance generally comes when the herd stops at midday, not really to eat but to rest their young calves.

During those first six or seven unlucky days, we were able to spot in the forest various duikers, of which there are a broad variety in the region. They are small and difficult animals to see and even more difficult to shoot with a rifle, as they are agile and wary. As soon as one gets down from the vehicle, they are off. Following a little way on foot, however, I was able with a quick offhand walking shot to take a western bush duiker and a good red-flanked duiker. I also took a lelwel hartebeest.

On the eighth day we set off in a different direction, to a spot where my French PH thought the elands might have moved. He was right. At dawn we found fresh spoor near a big salt lick. A large herd had obviously crossed the path not very long before and gone into the forest. This was the best chance that we had had yet, and we immediately jumped out of the vehicle and began following the tracks.

We followed for about five hours and finally caught up with them when they had stopped walking, probably to rest their young. Now the problem was getting near enough, first to choose a good bull among the herd and then to get a shot. After some glassing among the trees, we observed that there were two very similar good bulls. But the whole herd kept on moving, and the bull we chose kept on changing places with others. We had to keep on walking, trying to get ahead or broadside and not lose ground. And we had to be very careful as we approached, especially with the noisy leaves on the ground. If elands are startled by a noise or change of wind, they immediately break into a long trot—and that is the end of the hunt for that day.

The Ghost of the Forest

It had been hard to catch up with the herd, but now that we had there were still difficulties. A clear view of these

I took my giant eland in the forest-savanna. Note that the hole where the bullet penetrated diagonally can be seen in the middle of its flank. Central African Republic.

I rested during the day to avoid dehydration when I was lost in the savanna forest. Central African Republic.

animals is always a rarity, and a view of the entire body is even harder to come by, because the trees act as a kind of screen. To further confuse matters the females also have horns, although they are shorter. A big herd can be very hard to sort out.

When one finally does get into a position to shoot, the animals move on and the screen of trees hides the vital point for the shot. This frustrating situation demands a quick and precise shot if one is to take the so-called ghost of the forest. Some have said that it's like hunting an animal that weighs as much as a Cape buffalo, walks like a migrating caribou, and has the agility and well-developed senses of a greater kudu.

For this hunt I was using my Belgian Browning .375 Holland & Holland with a Zeiss telescopic 1½–6X scope. It was quite adequate for the range, which could be anywhere from 25 to 100 yards, possibly as much as 150 yards. Many times I was about to take a shot at my chosen bull, but it always moved on. Finally luck favored me and it stopped, just before crossing over from one spot in the forest to a kind of forest island. In that brief moment I was able to locate my bull, but it was at an angle to me. I couldn't see either its head or its tail: I was not sure which end was which. Finally it switched its tail, and I knew where the head was. A heart shot was impossible, though, because a tree was covering the spot. The eland was about one hundred yards away, and I had to make up my mind quickly. I decided on a shot that would enter its flank diagonally, aiming for the bullet to reach the lung and heart area in that way.

I held my breath and fired. The bull gave a big jump, ran off, and fell dead about forty paces away. All the party broke out in exclamations of congratulation. After all our exertions, the team was tremendously pleased. They put me on their shoulders and carried me in triumph toward the eland. It was a good trophy—not top class, but a very representative one and the best we had been able to find.

After photographs and celebrations came the time for skinning and cutting up the meat. Here I must explain that everybody in camp ate meat only when the client had shot an

This is a western bush duiker, my very first one. Central African Republic.

This Coleman container is filled with water from an elephant hole. I poured some into an empty plastic bottle and put two small water purifying tablets I found in the pocket of my canteen cover into it. Central African Republic.

animal. I had taken a northwestern savanna buffalo on my first hunting day, one week earlier. They are a little smaller than the Cape buffalo but larger than the dwarf forest buffalo. There had been no meat since then—which was a problem, because most of the men of the team and the assistants were in camp with their families, which of course had to be fed. When the hunting season ends, they walk to a region where they have small subsistence farms and then return at the beginning of the next season. One of the top men in the team, Jean, told me that his wife walked 125 miles to be with him at camp during hunting season. The Central African Republic is a very poor country.

In this case, the men wanted to take all of the meat when we left: They said they hadn't been fed enough during the past week. Of course a giant eland that weighs about a ton on the hoof must have about 1,300 pounds of meat. It was impossible to carry all of that back, even though our party consisted of the PH, the first and second hunters, and two assistants. Some would have to be left behind. After some discussion, however, the PH decided that he would return for the vehicle with one of the boys. A path could be cut to allow the Jeep in so that all of the meat could be taken away.

I couldn't argue with him, although it was not a normal procedure. This was his decision, and he was the head of the team. So off he went. The PH's headman began cutting his way up toward the place where he would meet the PH and the Jeep. Two men remained with me to do the skinning and cutting up of the meat. It had been a hot and strenuous day, so I sat myself down happily and as the hours went by I drank all the water in my canteen. And the two men did the same with their water. After all, the rest of the party would soon return, and we would drive off to camp.

Lost in the Savanna Forest

As night fell, we realized that the hunting car was not going to arrive that evening. Something had happened. They had

Assistant hunter Jean and I slept around this small fire while waiting for the rescue parties to find us. The carcass of giant eland can be seen at the far right. Central African Republic.

either lost their way or not been able to cut a pathway down to us. We would have to settle in for the night by ourselves. We built a fire to keep the hyenas away and got ready to spend the night about fifteen paces from the carcass of the giant eland. I asked Jean, who spoke good French, if this was a lion or leopard area. He said no, that although there were lions and leopards, their region was a little farther away. But there certainly would be hyenas. I had my two rifles with me, the .470 double and the .375.

Above all, though, I was feeling so thirsty that I really had no inclination to worry, move, or eat. There was plenty of meat from the eland, and if I had wanted we could have cooked some over the fire. But my mouth was dry and parched. Jean had a good idea: He got some blood from the heart of the eland and made me drink it, pouring it into my mouth. That helped a lot, because it freshened

The big tracks of the giant eland we found on the eighth day of the hunt were fresh, and we followed them until we caught up with the herd after five hours walking through the forest. Central African Republic.

my tongue, and at the same time it contained protein. So we settled in. Jean also made me a kind of bed of big leaves that he cut from the trees and laid alongside the fire. He lay on one side, I on the other. It was not long before there was a very good concert of hyena howling, which reminded me of my first experience in Kenya, with the cackling symphony of hyenas outside the tents. But they were cowardly and did not come too near the fire. We certainly didn't want them grabbing any of the meat, because that was what the boys of the team were planning to take to camp. We were hopeful that they would arrive the next morning.

The temperature at night was actually very pleasant, and I cannot say that at any moment I was cold during the night. When morning came we began to wonder why our party didn't arrive and what had happened. And this went on all day. I decided that I should keep still so as not to dehydrate. I had no desire to eat, but felt only a growing thirst. My tongue and mouth were dry and parched and a bit swollen. Jean found a shady place for me nearby where I lay all day, without moving, to avoid dehydration.

We realized that, as all the hunting camps communicated by radio, by now the main camp and all the others must have heard the news that we had not returned to camp and that something had happened. The hunting cars themselves did not have any means of radio communication, however. We imagined that a search would probably have begun for us—and that is actually what happened. Search parties went out, but it is amazing how the savanna forest goes on for miles and miles and looks all alike; there's hardly a point that can be differentiated from another.

As the story was retold to me afterward, my PH had got himself lost while looking for us. I remember that I had asked my PH if he had a GPS (global positioning system) with him, and he had said that, unfortunately, his was broken and not functioning. If he had had his GPS with him and had marked the position where the eland had been shot, he would have had no difficulty in finding his way back to us.

By the way he answered my question about the GPS, though, I realized that he never used it much. In all my African safaris I have never seen the PHs, the guides, or their trackers get lost, even when returning to camp at night. But they generally went back the same way they had gone out, and their sixth sense of direction never failed them. This time it was different. The French PH had had no trouble in finding his way back to the vehicle, but he was then going to try to return to us from a completely different direction, through a part of a forest he had not crossed before. So when his headman failed to cut a pathway up to meet him, he was completely lost.

In the meantime Jean had asked permission from me to go and see if he could find some water and take my .375 with him. He went off with an empty Coleman water container, and after quite a few hours I heard a shot: Obviously he had lost his way back, so I fired off my double and he showed up shortly afterward. But shots from farther away would have been drowned out by the forest; sounds do not travel far there. The water he brought back in the container was so filthy it had obviously come out of some local stream. I would not drink it, in spite of his insistence. Years ago I had had intestinal trouble from having drunk apparently good water that was bad, and I was not going to do that again, despite my thirst.

We spent the second night just like the first. I couldn't even eat some biscuits that I had with me in a small box. On the second morning Jean again went out to try to find water and came back with some from an elephant hole—that is, the hole that results from an elephant's footsteps when the ground is muddy and soft in the rainy season. This one had filled up with rainwater that, although a grayish color, was clearer than the first water had been.

I remembered that in my canteen cover there was a little bottle of U.S. Army water purification tablets that I had had for twenty years. I used them anyway, and took a small drink and washed my mouth out.

The second day went by with no news. I again spoke things over with Jean, insisting that it was best not to move. I knew that there would be search parties out, and if we moved we

Jean looks at the elephant hole filled with rain water that he found for me to drink when our party lost us for two days in the savanna forest. Central African Republic.

might make it only more difficult for them to find us. And in the process I would probably become weak and dehydrated. I had heard many stories about people getting lost and then walking in circles trying to find their way back. Many had died of exhaustion or dehydration.

Rescued by the Search Parties

On the third morning rescue suddenly appeared. Toward midmorning we heard a shot, and I immediately answered with another. Then the search party arrived. Of course there was a lot of embracing and celebrating. Eduardo Gerlero, who had hunted his eland in more or less the same area, was among them. He had been fortunate to have taken his on the first day, but he was lucky only in a way—because he had missed the strenuous exertion and anxiety of the hunt. He and his PH were with the first search party that arrived. There was another party, one that had come from the main camp, and they had brought not only water but also a sort of soup and some other food for me, as well as an orange drink.

Everything ended happily. The first rescue party had opened a path for the vehicle to come through, and eventually we were able to climb on board. Of course we took my trophy. It's incredible, but my hunting party still insisted on taking all the eland meat. But after two days in the sun I was sure it would not be fit to eat—and so it proved.

There was a big celebration party when be got back, in which all the people, all the locals, the members of our team and their wives, and all the camp members held a special dance in our honor. They brought out their drums and filled empty Coca-Cola cans with stones and tied them to their knees. They danced, and it made a sound like a tin band. It was quite a party. They asked for a speech, and I spoke to them in French, which they all understood. I thanked them for all their support, and then the dancing resumed. The whole camp was around the fire, dancing, and it was a sight. Then they all came up and shook hands with me, and it was interesting to see these people of a happy nature, simple and friendly, celebrating my safe return.

Chapter 14

Licht-Nicht, Licht-Nicht

One of the most special trophies that I have hunted is not a big-game animal, although it really is such because of the way it is hunted and its difficulty. It is a very special sort of wild bird, a big cock. There are two sorts. One is the capercaillie, the better known of the two, with its beautiful tail spread out like a fan. Its Latin name is *Tetrao urogallus,* and it is nearly as big as a turkey, weighing a little over fifteen pounds. The females are smaller and have their nests on the ground.

The other is called the lyre cock because its tail is in the form of a lyre. In Latin it is *Lylurus tetrix.* It's a little smaller than the capercaillie, perhaps from a third to a half its size. It lives in mountainous regions in Europe, especially France, Austria, Germany, Poland, Finland, and Norway.

The two are colored similarly—black with bluish petroleum reflections and a little white on the tail. The difference between them is that the capercaillie has a large, round tail that fans out, and it is larger in body. It stands on the branch of a tree, from where it crows its special call during the mating season. That is when they are hunted. It is a very alert bird, and the only time the hunter can get a shot at it is at sunrise, when it emits the mating call, which is quite long and loud, while standing on a branch in the forest. During that moment it can't hear or see anything. The hunter creeps up little by little, moving only while it is calling. This goes on and on until he can finally get a shot. It's considered a very difficult hunt.

The other bird, the lyre cock, is perhaps the rarer of the two. It's smaller, and it's quite different because it doesn't do its mating ritual in trees or in the middle of the forest. It mates rather high up on the slopes of snowbound mountains. It's a rare trophy animal, and few people have the opportunity of hunting one. I'm the only Argentine I know of in modern times who has had this wonderful chance. And it occurred in the middle of the Alpine region of Europe.

Roebucks in Bavaria

While I was touring various countries in Europe, partly on business and partly to get in a little hunting, I received two hunting invitations for a long weekend. One was to hunt roebuck, that small and alert deer typical of Europe and so popular because it is difficult to hunt: The hunter can get a quick shot only in the middle of the forest or in the clearings. A friend and I had been invited to the Castle of Tunzenberg about one hour north of Munich, in the south of Bavaria. I was fortunate and took two very nice roebuck; one of them brought a gold medal. It was a wonderful experience and great fun. I had never hunted roebuck before.

The horns of the roebuck are thick, spiky, and short. It's a small animal, with a shoulder height of around two to three feet and weighing around 90 pounds. And it is a difficult shot. It comes out only in the evenings or early morning in the forest clearings, and it is very wary. One has to be absolutely silent, and when the little animal stops to eat, the hunter has just one chance for a shot. I was very fortunate.

While I was there I got a call from another friend, Ottokarl, an important Austrian banker and hunter. He invited me to finish my short, three-day hunting holiday with the unique experience of hunting the lyre cock. I confess I had never heard of it. I knew about the capercaillie, but I had never heard of the lyre cock. I jumped at the idea.

Licht-Nicht, Licht-Nicht

Hunting the Lyre Cock in Austria

Ottokarl kindly sent a car for me, and I was driven from Munich to an Austrian hunting lodge in the province of Styria, a little south of Linz and west of Salzburg. It was in the middle of the Alpine mountain and lake region—beautiful, wonderful scenery. As this was early spring, the mountains were still covered with snow, and the big pines and cedars were especially striking.

I arrived in the evening at an old game lodge that had been established during the days of Emperor Franz Joseph of the Austro-Hungarian Empire. There was a nice lodge, and the hunting area went a long way up into the mountains—it was a large area with cabins where one might spend the night. The hunting was mainly for red deer, roebuck, and chamois. The Austrian and I became very good friends, and in later years he twice invited me back to hunt chamois. But my first hunt in the area was for lyre cock, of which I knew absolutely nothing.

It was a great privilege to be invited to hunt lyre cock. This game lodge had a quota of only six cocks a year. They were very strict and invited only people who they knew would not wound an animal, because they were so rare. Before going up the mountain they tested the hunter under the pretext of lending him a gun, in order to see him shoot at a target. The guns were over-unders, the top barrel being a shotgun and the bottom a rifle.

Of course, I would not choose to use a shotgun to shoot a sitting bird. With a rifle it's more of a challenge. These were small-caliber rifles, one being a .222 and the other a .243. They told me that in the past they used to use full-metal jacket bullets so that they wouldn't expand. The idea was to avoid spoiling the trophy; if the body was damaged, there was no trophy. They found, however, that hunters were wounding a lot of birds by not placing the shot precisely; with a full-metal case the bullet just went through. If it didn't hit a vital spot, the animal flew off, wounded.

In recent years they had begun using a softpoint, a softnose bullet—that is, an expanding bullet. There is a greater chance of getting a kill, but also a greater danger of destroying the

Outside the log cabin with my lyre cock and the Austrian jaeger. *Austria.*

trophy. The shot itself is a sitting shot, from between fifty and one hundred yards, if shooting with a rifle. The shotgun barrel is used for a flying shot, should there be one.

This form of hunting goes back many years. Before taking you up the mountain they explain the shot with the help of a little drawing, a side view of the bird. They point out a small circle in the stomach area that is the only spot to shoot at. The expanding bullet, if placed anywhere else, will destroy the body of the bird. One has a very tiny target, and one either misses it, hits it, or destroys the trophy. That's why they are so strict about whom they will let up. They test the hunter on a 100-yard range, and with the excuse of trying which rifle fits best they get a chance to see if he can put a bullet in the center of the target. I did, with both rifles, and then chose the one that I felt more comfortable with.

I had arrived at the lodge with just enough light for the shooting test. About 9:00 P.M. we started to climb up the mountain. The people who knew how to ski used skis, but they lent me some snowshoes. It was a beautiful night, and we had a four-hour climb. Everything was white with the snow, and the pine and cedar trees looked black in the night. It was a most impressive scene to witness under a full moon.

The altitude here was about 4,500 to 6,000 feet: This wasn't one of the highest peaks of the Alps. We arrived about 1:00 A.M., and there was a small cabin in which my friend, who was accompanying me, stayed as an observer. There was also the professional hunter, in German called a *jaeger*. He could speak only German, which I don't know, but Ottokarl, himself a good hunter, spoke both English and German and explained the procedure. One had to hide under a big fir or cedar tree and wait for the right moment, which was about an hour before sunrise. Then the mating ritual began, and it was necessary to be very quiet. It meant a long wait in the cold, and my friend stayed in the cabin.

The Mating Ritual

I went with the *jaeger* to our post, the hideout, under a big tree and waited until the females came down onto a sort of flat

In the courtyard of Tunzemberg Castle with my gold-medal roebuck. Bavaria, Germany.

The Lord Derby or giant eland was the last of the Big Three of the spiral-horned antelope that I took. Central African Republic.

On our return to camp after hunting the giant eland, the whole staff flocked to us, throwing flowers and branches with leaves on the hunting car and chanting their typical song. Central African Republic.

I took this black savanna buffalo on the first day of my Central African hunt. Central African Republic.

When I took this puma with a handgun after the chase, it was surrounded by the dogs. Argentina.

This collared peccary received a South American Major Award from Safari Club International and ranks sixth in its record book.

I hunted my first chamois in the Alpine mountains of the Province of Styria, in the same area where there is a game lodge that was established during the days of Franz-Joseph of the Austro-Hungarian Empire. Austria.

The head alone on my heavily broomed High Altai argali weighed 55 pounds. Mongolia.

Three generations of sport hunters, passing on the tradition: My grandson José is shown with a free-range axis deer that was his first game trophy, together with his father José, brother Alejandro, and myself. Argentina.

My grandson Alejandro took his blackbuck free range with his father José, again passing on the family tradition. Province of Buenos Aires, Argentina.

My third son Tom, who was hunting blackbuck free range in the Province of Buenos Aires, was a passionate and knowledgeable wildlife lover. Argentina.

I used a handgun to take this white-lipped peccary. Northern hunting area, Argentina.

I took my best brown brocket deer in the northern region of the country. It ranks seventh in SCI's record book, and it received a South American Major Award. Argentina.

My best blackbuck still ranks number ten in SCI's Record Book of Trophy Animals. *Province of Buenos Aires, Argentina.*

mountainside of snow—hard snow, because it is quite high up. About ten hens landed and began walking around. After a while, four males landed. And then the mating ritual began.

The males began their mating call, a guttural sound like *rrr, rrr, rrr*, which was beautiful to hear under the full moon. And then they began their ritual dance. They seemed to skate around like ballet dancers and opened their wings. As they skated around the females, they were probably observing which were receptive to their attentions. I would have loved to have had a video camera with a sound recorder to capture this extraordinary scene.

The ritual went on for about half an hour, during which time I had to wait, first for there to be enough light and then to try to pick out the biggest male. Next it was a matter of following the bird through the scope of the rifle, trying to fix upon that little circle in the lower part of the body that was the target.

Licht? - Nicht, Licht? - Nicht

One was supposed to hold off shooting until it was light enough to be certain of a good shot. This was where I got entangled with my German, because light is *licht*. I kept on asking my *jaeger* if there was enough light, asking him to advise me. And he kept on saying, "*Nicht*," which is "no"—meaning wait. So it was, *"Licht?"* "*Nicht.*" *"Licht?"* *"Nicht,"* until I was not sure if I was right or wrong or what the German meant. In the end I took it upon myself to decide when there was enough light for me to get my shot off.

The small rifle had a telescopic sight, which I found difficult to use in the moonlight. I don't like shooting at night, and normally I don't—except in these out-of-the-ordinary circumstances. We were posted about seventy-five yards from where those incredible birds had landed and were staging their ballet dance as a mating ritual.

I at last centered on one male and had to decide when the light was good enough for me to make the shot. It was a very small point to aim at, and the bird was skating all the time. I would have to wait for it to stop a moment and then get the shot off in the right place, that very small circle, within half a second or so. That was my problem. But in the end I finally decided the time had come. There was enough light.

I centered my attention on the cock, and suddenly it stood still. I fired, and to my great relief it dropped, stone dead. It was a clean shot, well placed. And I, of course, immediately jumped up and wanted to go and see, but the *jaeger* caught me by my arm and pulled me back. "*Nicht*," he said, meaning, "No, don't move." Extraordinarily enough, the other birds had not noticed the one that had fallen. They hadn't even heard the shot. Or if they had, it had not disturbed them. Incredible.

They went on with their ritual ballet dance. I had to let them go on, and not disturb them, until they had finished. And when it was over they flew off to the outskirts of the surrounding forest and stayed on the limbs of trees for half an hour to an hour more until it got completely light and the sun had risen. Then they flew off. Only at that point did the *jaeger* allow me to go out and see what I had shot. After shooting the lyre cock I had had to wait about three hours—a very impatient wait.

It was cold—very cold. I had taken my little whiskey flask with me, as always, but it was cold nevertheless. All that time, the bird never moved. When I finally did see it, it was a wonderful sight: a black bird nearly as big as a small turkey with a red crest, a beautiful lyre-shaped tail, and the sun reflecting off its glossy feathers. All in all, the hunting itself hadn't taken very long—it was all over in one night and one morning. But the incredible way in which it all took place, the extraordinary scenery, and the unbelievable ritual ballet dance were like nothing I had ever seen before. It was a real highlight in my amateur hunting career. After it was all over we walked down the mountain and received the normal congratulations that await the successful hunter. They were waiting for me with a big breakfast and a lot of toasting with strong spirits. I was very proud of my lyre cock.

My Trophy

To describe the lyre cock, I would say that it weighs about nine pounds. They feed in the forest on what birds generally feed on—insects, small mice, or things like that. They live in the forest but come out to mate in the open. That's quite different from the capercaillie, which lives entirely in the forest and does not leave it. But the lyre cock comes flying out of the forest at high altitudes, higher than the capercaillie, because their mating is done out in the open. It happens only once a year, and the mating season lasts about a month. I was really very lucky to have been there at the right moment and to have taken one of these very special quota birds.

The jaeger *with his dog and the lyre cock in his right hand, walking down the mountainside back to the main hunting lodge. Austria.*

According to the tradition, these birds have never been domesticated, and they are not bred artificially. They are not like pheasants, which are shot after being bred to maintain their numbers. That's why so much care is taken with them: They are completely wild. The birds are under government supervision, and on private property there are quotas controlling how many can be shot every year, according to a census that is kept.

The birds would probably be endangered if there was complete liberty, but as it is, they're not easy to get access to. For one thing, the land is private. One can't climb up that mountain without an invitation from the owners. And, too, there is such a short period during the year when hunting is possible. During the rest of the time, it often seems impossible even to see them.

The lyrebirds mate on the mountainside year after year, more or less in the same place. When my friends took me up they knew exactly the place where the birds would be. We didn't have to search for them. They knew that those birds would be coming down at that place, and they chose the tree under which we would hide, some fifty to one hundred yards away. It was an extraordinary experience.

Chapter 15

On a Mokoro in the Okavango Delta

A few years ago two good friends of mine, pleased to have completed a successful business venture with my help, asked me to organize a safari to Africa—a real old-time tented safari. And each of us would take one of our sons. That was their invitation to me.

It was a wonderful opportunity, and they told me to choose the country. I chose Botswana. Kenya, of course, had closed hunting; it had been out since 1977. I knew that Botswana, on the other hand, was one of the places where a real old-fashioned sort of safari with a tented camp could still be had. Many of the best PHs had migrated there from Kenya.

Sporting International and Safari South were prominent outfitters in those days, and I happened to know one of their directors, Frank Green, with whom I corresponded regularly. I asked him to organize this hunt with three of his top professionals. Each of them would take out a father and son, meaning two clients for each professional. It was a great idea and sounded like it would be lots of fun.

Failure of the Projected Hunt in Botswana

The hunt was organized about a year in advance. It was scheduled for June 1990, which was the right time of the year to go. It so happened that after everything was arranged, however, about two months before the date of departure, I got a telephone call from my friends saying, look, something

The reedbuck is a beautiful trophy and a sporting hunt in the long grass of the delta area. Okavango Delta, Botswana.

has turned up. It turned out that there was a very important business meeting that they had to attend in Europe. They had to cancel the safari.

The meeting was to be about a week before the safari. They told me that this was going to be an important turning point in their professional careers, that it was going to open a new horizon for their business. They were terribly disappointed, but they told me to go ahead. The invitation still stood. I could get two other friends to go along with me and go anyway. Of course I didn't accept, because the fun was going with them. So I said no. If they didn't go, I wouldn't go either.

It was all very disappointing, and everybody felt frustrated, including the safari company and the three PHs. My friends had lost their 50 percent deposit on the hunt by canceling with such short notice, and the professionals were furious because they really couldn't understand why a business commitment had to interfere with such an exceptional safari.

As it turned out, two weeks after they had given me the news I got a very bad kidney colic. I was hunting with another two friends in the north of our country, far up in not too civilized surroundings. We returned one day sooner than planned because it was raining hard, and the morning of the next day I got a horrible pain in my side—apparently a kidney stone. Surgery was necessary, and I had a very bad time of it. I was fortunate not to lose my kidney. So it appeared that destiny had decided we should not go on that safari.

An Obsession for a Sitatunga, and a New Opportunity to Hunt

One of the important areas of Botswana, perhaps the most important, is the Okavango Delta. In it there is a special animal that is considered one of the top international trophies: the sitatunga. It is a semiaquatic spiral-horned antelope that is very difficult to see and hunt. I developed an obsession with this animal.

Since 1990, the whole hunting and outfitting scene in Botswana has changed. All of the concessions have been reallocated, and the hunting companies are mostly different. My friends of Safari South have disappeared from the map.

PH Don Price with head poler Rex and an assistant preparing the mekoro *to go out into the delta for the sitatunga hunt. Okavango Delta, Botswana.*

The two top professionals nowadays in Botswana are Jeff Rann and Johan Calitz. I knew them both, having met them at the annual conventions of the Safari Club International at Reno or Las Vegas. The one I got on with in a more friendly way was Johan Calitz.

I kept on asking him, from 1996 onward, year after year, when he was going to get a sitatunga quota for me. There is a strict quota system in Botswana, especially for the sitatunga, because it's a rare animal. Johan Calitz had only one sitatunga a year for his camp in the Okavango Delta that he could allot to a hunter. Finally, however, he told me that he had a quota for me for the year 2000. He notified me two years in advance. And I answered immediately: Done.

In the meantime an Argentine friend of mine, Eduardo Gerlero, who was a member of the board of directors of our Safari Club chapter in Argentina, was getting more and more enthusiastic about hunting. He very much wanted a lion quota, for which Botswana is one of the most important countries. But again, quotas were very restricted. I mentioned to Johan Calitz that I had a friend who would like to go with me, although he would be looking for lion.

Johan Calitz replied that it was a very difficult proposition, because he was allotting lion quotas three years in advance, and he had none available for the year in which I had my sitatunga quota. Nevertheless, I asked that my friend be kept in mind in the event of a cancellation. And about six months later we got a fax saying that there had indeed been a cancellation, and that the quota would be allotted to Eduardo Gerlero.

Botswana

Botswana is a very special country, and my safari there was one of the nicest I've ever had. Botswana is about the size of France but has only 1.5 million inhabitants. Its neighbor Zimbabwe, the former Southern Rhodesia, is about the same size, perhaps a little larger, and has 11.5 million inhabitants. That's one thing that makes it special.

A Nile crocodile at the water's edge under the papyrus and big reeds. Okavango Delta, Botswana.

The first inhabitants of Botswana are supposed to have been the Bushmen, who arrived 25,000 years ago. That's a long time ago—and they are still there. The Bushmen are hunters, and the few that remain now live in the middle of the Kalahari Desert. Later, much later, they were followed by other tribes, such as the Tswanas in the thirteenth century. That's where the name of the country comes from. And later on these Tswanas increased in number, especially in the seventeenth century, when they fled from the fierce Zulus a little farther south. They moved to the north and established a stable population there.

After the arrival of the British, the Tswanas and all the other tribes were joined by the Boers when they abandoned the Cape Colony. They left in that famous trek northward with all their wagons, their people, and their cattle. The name "Boer" comes from the Dutch meaning "farmer," and of course these were descendants of the first Dutch white settlers in Cape Town. But the Boers were a harsh people, and they were harsh with the native Tswanas.

At that time Britain's presence was already felt in Southern Africa, and the Tswanas asked for the protection of Queen Victoria against the Boer settlers. Of course the British Empire was only too pleased to add another jewel to its crown, because doing so opened a route from Cape Town to the mines in Central Africa. Cecil Rhodes had conquered what is now Zimbabwe and was then called Rhodesia. The Tswana land thus became the Protectorate of Bechuanaland.

A few years later in 1895, Cecil Rhodes applied pressure to try to get Bechuanaland absorbed into his company, the British South Africa Company, and wrest it from the British Colonial Department. In response, three of the tribal leaders of the Tswana people went to London to ask for the protection of Queen Victoria herself against Cecil Rhodes. And Queen Victoria gave Bechuanaland its autonomy.

Nearly a hundred years later, in 1986, the British gave Bechuanaland its freedom, and it took the name of Botswana. Its first prime minister and then president was a very well cultured man. He was later knighted and called Sir Seretse Khama, educated at Oxford, a fan of jazz and knowledgeable in literature and history. He had married an Englishwoman named Ruth Williams and was a grandson of one the tribal chiefs that had gone to London.

Sir Seretse Khama did a great job in Botswana because he kept it a peaceful and tolerant country, in which there was no racial or religious hatred and into which refugees from surrounding countries could flee. It has probably been the only country in Africa that has made a peaceful transition from being a protectorate or a colony to full independence. Khama's Democratic National Party is still in power.

It was not one of the most common hunting destinations in Africa. For one thing, it was very poor. After the discovery of copper, nickel, coal, and finally diamonds, however, economic development possibilities opened up, because concessions were awarded to foreign companies for the exploitation of those resources. And then came the tourist industry and the safari industry.

Hunting is now important for bringing foreign exchange into the country. The land is sparsely inhabited, mainly because of the desert and the delta. Four-fifths of the population occupy only one-fifth of the territory, and 80 percent of Botswana is taken up by the Kalahari Desert, the largest sand desert in the world. The Okavango Delta covers about 5,700 to 6,900 square miles, varying with the yearly rainfall in Angola that originates the floods. There are plains and forests in the Chobe area, a little to the north, and some pasture lands, and the desert. That's it.

Consequently, they have had to organize their natural resources. About 17 percent of the land has been established as game reserves and national parks. And even in the middle of the Kalahari Desert, which is enormous, they have established 19,300 square miles as a natural game reserve for the Bushmen. Farther to the southeast are the Makgadikgadi Pans. These used to be an enormous saltpan whose water has now dried up. Antelopes such as gemsbok and springbok, which can live with virtually no water, can be found there, as well as lions, leopards, and cheetahs, which get their fluid from the animals that they hunt.

The Okavango Delta

Botswana has the only inland delta in the world—the Okavango Delta. All other deltas, being at the outflow of a river, flow into the sea. This delta, however, does not. The Okavango River originates in Angola and flows down across the Caprivi Strip of Namibia, a very narrow strip at the north of Botswana. When the rainy season comes in Angola, from October to May, the river swells enormously and flows into Botswana through what is called the panhandle, which is about fifty miles long. It travels through a kind of ravine and then arrives at the plains, where it forms an enormous delta. The flooding originates about 3.5 billion cubic feet of water, and the delta gets this tremendous amount every six months. It gradually disappears in the sands of the Kalahari Desert.

This then is the only delta that does not run into the sea. But when it grows, when the water enters the delta, it's an amazing sight. There is an enormous influx of wildlife, great quantities and varieties of birds, fish, small animals, and big-game species such as elephant, buffalo, and semiaquatic antelope. This is a big swamp, but it is not a muddy swamp. It's a beautiful, clear-water swamp. The main canals, which run like hairpin U-turns, are about nine feet deep, although the volume of water varies with the seasons.

There are a lot of crocodiles and hippopotamuses here. Hippos cannot be hunted, however, because they keep the main canals free of the underwater growth of vegetation. They clear the canals as they move through them with their tremendous bodies.

Maun is what is called the capital of the safari industry, because it is right on the limit of the Okavango Delta. Maun is where all the safari expeditions into the delta leave from, either by a four-wheel-drive vehicle or by airplane. It's a small town with not more than about twenty thousand inhabitants, and it is a typical "Far West" cluster of houses. All the outfitters have their offices there, and a lot of photographic safaris also originate there.

Aerial view of the delta taken from our small charter plane on our way from Maun to camp. Okavango Delta, Botswana.

The wife of one of the camp members offering me some freshly baked bread. The people were very friendly. Okavango Delta, Botswana.

All hunting is done from dugout canoes, called a *mokoro* or *mekoro* (plural) in the local language. This dugout canoe needs an explanation. It's a very flimsy craft, about nine feet long but very narrow—perhaps less than three feet wide. It's propelled by either one or two men, not using oars but poles. They are punters. Generally one of them stands on the back and the other in the bow.

Riding in such a dugout, it's normal to see big papyrus, as in photos of the Nile in Egypt. It's a beautiful sight when the papyrus is in flower and the *mokoro* goes in among them silently. There are no noises of civilization, not even a motorboat. Punting out begins from just before sunrise and moves pretty slowly.

It's quite chilly early in the morning, but as the day goes on it gets warmer. By the time the sun is out one is in shirtsleeves. It's a very nice climate. In the swamp outside of the deep canals there are crocs that move very silently in the water. I remember once that one was heading straight toward us. We could barely see its eyes and nostrils, and the head poler just gave it a knock on the snout. Off it went. We were not hunting crocs: We were looking for sitatunga.

There are big islands along the way, where the different sorts of antelope graze, and their tracks can be seen in the sand. Or one may run into them on the island. One can have a picnic on an island and rest during the middle of the day. And in the right season there are a lot of elephant and buffalo on these islands, too. It's really an extraordinary place for wildlife.

Hunting the Sitatunga

The sitatunga is considered one of the top international trophies. It can be hunted in several ways. I hunted mine from a *mokoro*. Many days can go by before the hunter finds a sitatunga among the reeds and papyrus, where it spends most of the time eating with half its body under the water. It is a very good swimmer, having elongated hooves to help it swim and walk on the reeds. When one appears, the hunter has to stand up in the *mokoro*, which is narrow, try to get his balance, and fire. In addition to the difficulties presented by standing in a dugout, the sitatunga is hard to see among the reeds.

Another way to hunt sitatunga is as they do in Zambia and some West African countries—from a high platform or tree that looks over the reeds in the swamp. Early in the morning or late in the evening, a sitatunga may be seen coming out among the reeds. It is generally a very long shot. However, I don't find it much fun waiting up for hours, sitting or standing on a platform. Cruising in the *mokoro,* on the other hand, is a pleasure.

A third way to hunt sitatunga is by using pleasure cruisers, which is what they do on the Chobe River, in the north of Botswana. These are medium-size cruisers with platforms on them. The people who want to shoot stand on these platforms while the boat goes slowly along one of the main canals. On either side there are the swamps, and if the hunter gets a shot it is generally a long one. But standing on a high platform in a boat going along a canal is not the same as being in a dugout

Here I am with PH Don Price and his hunting team after an exciting hunt for red lechwe in the middle of the delta swamp. Okavango Delta, Botswana.

With PH Don Price and a gold-medal tsessebe taken on firm land in the area. Okavango Delta, Botswana.

canoe in the middle of the swamp, in the midst of nature. I would say that one of the nicest things I've ever done in my life was searching for sitatunga in a *mokoro* among the reeds and papyrus.

Incredibly, on the very first day, about 9:00 A.M., the head poler, Rex the punter, abruptly stopped the *mokoro*, put in the pole, and began to look intensely among the reeds. His eyes could see what ours could not.

There in the reeds was a very good sitatunga. I couldn't see it. Suddenly my PH saw it, and he said, "Look, look. At ten o'clock. There he is." But by the time I saw it, it was off. And apparently it had been a really good one, so everybody was feeling bad. But not me. If I had shot my sitatunga after my first three hours in the delta, my hunt would have ended too soon. I preferred to get a poorer trophy but have the pleasure of spending a week searching the swamp.

One goes out each day at 6:00 A.M. and comes back at 6:00 P.M. At night we would return to a tent in a very nice camp. Every minute of this hunting experience is enjoyable. Just being poled around, in silence, trying to pierce the reeds with one's eyes, looking at the birds and the scenery, is a pleasure.

Rex, the head hunter, at camp making a new mokoro*— with an impressive display of precision. Okavango Delta, Botswana.*

It begins to get dark at 6:00, and that is when the punters must be very careful. They don't like to come back when it's very dark, because they might run into a hippo on one of the main canals. Trouble can result, because if the hippo gets hit or scared, it can easily overturn the *mokoro*. And they do get mad. And nasty. In fact, hippos cause more fatalities in Africa than any other animal, even land animals.

On the seventh day of my hunt there was nice weather, although a bit clouded. It was then that we finally saw a good sitatunga. The animal was about one hundred yards away, and Rex was, of course, the first to see it. He was standing on the front of the *mokoro*, which he stopped by sticking the pole into the bottom. He made signs for us to be quiet, because the sitatunga has a wonderful sense of hearing.

I got up and saw it. At first, I had to get my balance with the heavy rifle in my hands. I was using the .375, because a heavy bullet that can penetrate the reeds is what's needed. I grabbed the pole sticking out of the mud and put my left hand on it to steady the rifle. I got off a good shot, and the sitatunga went down.

I immediately jumped out of the canoe with the water just under my knees. It was cold but I didn't feel it. I rushed up to the sitatunga. We were all excited, because this is not an easy animal to find, not an easy animal to see, and not an easy animal to shoot. Mine did not have exceptionally long horns, but it was a very good representative trophy. It was not as good as the one that got away on that first day, but to me it was more valuable for the experience it gave me in the Okavango Delta.

This marked the completion of my hunt for the spiral-horned antelope of Africa. I had taken a Menelik bushbuck in Ethiopia and a Chobe bushbuck in Southern Zimbabwe, where Don Price, my PH, had a concession. On that latter occasion I also had the opportunity of shooting a crocodile, which is challenging because it requires a very precise shot. It's an animal one doesn't generally think about hunting, but I had read how special it was to hunt crocodile. They are generally taken when basking in the sun at midday, on the bank of a river.

One day, while hunting the bushbuck, we saw two good crocs, one a little bigger than the other. I had read that you must never wound a crocodile, because in that case it will crawl into the water and the current of the river will sweep it away. And then the trophy is lost. One must take it with one shot. It's not a question of a brain shot, because the brain is very small, the size of a golf ball, and it's in a very difficult place to get at because of the bones on the side of his head. Only if the croc is coming straight at you can one get a brain shot. From land the best shot is where the lips end. There's a sort of smile, just about an inch above the end of which is where the vertebrae of the spine join up with the head. If you can hit that spot, the spinal cord will be cut.

One must be very quiet. The first croc we were able to creep up to was on the opposite bank, and I was able to shoot it neatly. Its companion slipped into the river and apparently drifted off. So my PH told his boys, "Well, now you cross over there and bring the dead croc back." They were rather anxious, because they were not quite sure if its companion had really gone off or if it was still nearby. But it had gone, so they went in. They took the dead croc by the tail and brought it back across the river. It turned out to be a very nice one.

I ended my hunt in the Okavango with another semiaquatic antelope, the red lechwe. It is rather similar to the sitatunga, although more abundant and of a different family. One sees more of them, and they are a little easier to find. But they are very beautiful as they rush through the swamp, jumping and splashing. On land I took a tsessebe, that rather ungainly antelope, but very fast and with beautiful skin, chestnut brown with black on its shoulders, hindquarters, and face. I also hunted reedbuck and steenbok, the smallest of them all in the long grass. It was an interesting safari because they were all difficult shots and quite different from anything else I had done before.

At the same time that I was hunting in the delta, my friend Eduardo Gerlero had gone to the Chobe area and there successfully took a very good lion, after nearly walking his legs off tracking it, and then also a good elephant, stopping a frontal charge with his double Jeffery .475 No. 2. We then

Standing up in the mokoro *to shoot a sitatunga with my Browning .375 and 1.5–6X42mm Zeiss riflescope. Okavango Delta, Botswana.*

met in the delta, where he took a red lechwe and a tsessebe. On our return to Maun, the evening before we left, we had a nice dinner with Johan Calitz, who flew in from another camp for the purpose.

To conclude, I would say that to hunt in the Okavango Delta is one of the most extraordinary of experiences and a great privilege. I would recommend that anyone go there, even if not to hunt but just to have the pleasure of spending a few days in a *mokoro* in direct contact with nature. The Okavango, the so-called jewel of the Kalahari, is an amazing land, full of life when it is flooded with water. It's a paradise for wildlife and for conservation, and a very special place to hunt. It was one of my most memorable and pleasurable safaris.

Chapter 16

Closing Remarks

Many times I have been asked why I hunt. It is a good question, and it can have either a simple answer or a more profound one. The simple answer is that I like it. But beyond that, I always remember something written by the famous Spanish philosopher José Ortega y Gasset (1883–1955), who in 1942 wrote the prologue to the memoirs of the Count of Yebes's, *Twenty Years of Big Game Hunting*. Ortega's introduction contained a host of profound comments and reflections, becoming almost a treatise on hunting all by itself.

One of his reflections that most impressed me, and one that best explains true hunters, is that the important thing about hunting is the moments one spends hunting. What one most likes is "to be" hunting. The important thing about the hunt is "to be hunting," whether one kills or not. Killing is secondary. One doesn't hunt to kill. One kills because one is hunting, as a consequence.

Hunting, in my judgment, is part of one's way of life. For someone who loves nature, who loves animals, all sorts of animals, among them wild animals, it's one of the best ways of being inside nature and close to the animals. I haven't found a better way. And in doing so, of course one loves nature. One doesn't want to spoil nature. One respects the habitat in which one is hunting, and one also loves the animals that are hunted, which at first sight seems to be a contradiction.

How can one shoot something that one loves? But really there is no contradiction. Inside every man—and I think this comes from his ancestral background—there is a challenge that goes back to the times when our forefathers, ages ago, had to hunt to live. In sport hunting nowadays some people like to eat the meat they take, but that is not the purpose of my hunting. Mine is trophy hunting, which I think is the real sport hunting. But the main thing about it is the challenge.

There grows up between the hunter and those animals he loves a challenge in which he pits his wits against their instincts, because the animals have, as we must recognize, much better developed senses of scent, hearing, and vision than does civilized man. On the other hand, man has developed a technology—precise and powerful rifles and binoculars and telescopic sights that compensate us for our natural inferiority.

When it comes to the act of hunting, it is said that the real hunter must get as near as possible to the animal to show that he is skilled enough to take the animal on its own grounds. That is true, but it is also not always possible. In a mountainous region there may be a big crevasse or gully that cannot be crossed, and on the other side an important trophy that the hunter may have sought for days. Then he must also be a good shot.

The hunter must be a perfectionist. He must be able to use the best of his wits as a good tracker, to approach the animal in its own surroundings, respecting the natural world it is in, and also to make the best use of the weapons he has. If he is going to kill, he must be capable of making a clean kill so that the animal does not suffer. A hunter who is a bad shot ends up with an animal that runs off wounded. Perhaps it will not be found and suffers, and that's sad. So one of the main principles of ethical hunting is to try never to wound an animal, but always to make a clean kill.

The more the hunter knows about the animals he hunts, the more he loves them, and the more he respects them. One respects the animals that are being hunted, and that ensures that one not take unfair advantage of them, because that would not be respecting them. When one has killed an animal sometimes one feels sorry, but there comes a point in the challenge when there is no going back. One must complete the challenge and must be the victor, although love and respect for the animal are still there.

The best trophies are normally old individuals that have been ousted from the herd because their reproductive life is over. Their elimination is in accord with the principles of conservation, as it helps to maintain the necessary balance between the availability of forage and the number of animals in the population. That is why a hunter will always choose an old individual, and not a young one.

In addition, it must be an animal that has required from the hunter as much effort as possible in hunting it, one that inspires the victor's sense of triumph. But if at the moment when one should pull the trigger the hunter realizes that the sense of honest accomplishment is not present, one should not fire. In the end it is the enjoyment of the hunt, not the killing, that matters. And that is part of the ethics of hunting.

Ethical Hunting

A lot is said about the ethics of hunting, but sometimes it is not adequately explained. I consider that the essence of ethics is always to play straight, never to take unfair advantage of an opponent. That is what the British ingrained in all their sporting traditions: fair play. And it does not matter if the hunter is alone and no one will see. Fair play is the essence of ethics. Ortega y Gasset put it this way: "At the moment of truth, the hunter only has as witnesses God and his conscience."

Characteristics of a Good Hunter

The complete hunter should be able to perform well in all geographic regions and climatic conditions. He must be a good hunter on the plains, where the animals can see him from far off and where a careful approach is crucial. In the bush or thick forest the shot won't be the same, and the approach will also vary. High in the mountains a lot of climbing may be required, and a lot of endurance. And in all cases, much patience is required. The hunter must not mind if it takes hours, days, or weeks to find his quarry, and sometimes he will come home without it—perhaps to return another year if he really wants it. That has happened many times in international hunts.

The hunter must prepare himself. He must prepare his character, and he must prepare his weapons. There is a great deal more to it than simply picking up a rifle and going out shooting. A real hunter must absorb a lot of information, and if he really loves nature he will have informed himself of the animals and their habitat by reading and by listening to those who have gone before him. He must also be humble when he has finally attained his trophy, not like some I have seen on hunting videos.

The hunter must learn to be a good winner as well as a good loser. And a good winner recognizes his personal triumph without making too much of it. There may have been an element of luck involved, or a lot of people may have helped. And at the same time, there is the respect for the animal that has been such a good opponent and has made possible such a good hunt. All of this makes up what I would say is the complex world of a hunter who thinks of himself as a true hunter, and acts that way.

Memorable Hunts

Memorable hunts are created by many factors, one of which is certainly the exertion the hunter had to undergo—how much real effort was necessary, and how much heat, cold, thirst, hunger, or lack of sleep was involved. My wife has always told me when she sees me go off hunting, "You are a masochist. You like to flail yourself." But this is not flailing myself. It's a challenge. It's a pleasure that sweeps the cobwebs out of one's mind and substitutes other ideas and preoccupations. The hunter may be suffering physically, but he is enjoying it mentally. And it also puts him on a spiritually higher grade, if he understands it that way.

A second factor would be the difficulty of finding the trophy, or the animal's dangerous character. Some animals are simply harder to find, without meaning that they are endangered.

Perhaps the habitat they are in is more difficult to reach. Then they are more difficult to, in a word, prey upon.

Of course, many animals prey upon each other, and as such they have well-honed skills of escape and defense. And in the process of hunting them we must return to the concept of fair play. There comes a moment in which the animal must have a chance to escape or to attack the hunter. That is the famous 50-50 percent rule that the British established in Africa. If it is a dangerous animal that charges or that can attack, it must have that chance. The hunter must not try to shoot an elephant, for example, from one hundred yards with a telescopic sight. He must go up to twenty yards, near the elephant or lion or buffalo, and shoot it on its own ground, on its own terrain—not from a high seat or blind where he is out of danger, or from a vehicle, in which case the animal can't smell the human scent.

Some people even enjoy enticing the animal into a charge, thereby putting themselves at risk. I think that is sporting, also. This is the difference, I would say, between a sporting hunter and a hunter who is out simply for the kill and has no respect for himself or for the animals he hunts. And this is also an element in a memorable hunt. Animals that are easy to hunt have much less value as a challenge.

Apart from these considerations, in my judgment some trophies, because of their impressive nature—because the animal is so majestic, because it is so beautiful—have a value in and of themselves as trophies. One could mention the elephant's tusks, the lion and its mane, the buffalo's boss and horns, or the wonderful spiral-horned antelope. These trophies have a value in themselves because of their inherent significance.

Passing on the Tradition

At the same time, the hunter must try to set an example for younger hunters. There are associations like the Safari Club International, the International Council for Hunting and Conservation, and hunting and conservation clubs, by means of which the hunter can pass on his experience to the young, and sometimes take them out hunting with him. By these means the hunter is passing the tradition on to the next generation—be it his sons, his grandsons, or to friends. He is passing on his own experiences so that what he has learned will live on after him.

Photographic Safaris

Photographic safaris have about half the challenges of a hunting safari. I've done it myself. I've also tried to do both at the same time, which is not always possible. While I hunt I normally take a lot of photos, and if one does that by itself—that's a photographic safari—I think that it comes very near to hunting, if it's done the right way. I'm not thinking here of the herds of people who get into tourist cars or minivans and go off to a game park to look at the animals from a distance. If one does it from a hunting car with a real guide, and gets near the animals, that's much like a real hunt. The essence is to get up near to the animals in their own habitat and feel the excitement and the challenge of taking the photos. There will be one element, however, that will probably be lacking, and that is the danger of exposure to an animal that may come at the hunter during a hunt. But for the rest, I think that good photographic safaris have many of the same qualities as hunting safaris.

Three Famous Hunters

One of the most famous men in the history of hunting was Frederick Selous (1851–1916). He was something of the model of the British Victorian explorer and hunter who had all the principles and assets that I have mentioned. He was a great hunter who could put up with immense hardships and who accomplished many noteworthy objectives. He is one of the archetypes of hunting.

Alongside him we may place the famous "Karamojo" Bell (Walter D. M. Bell, 1880–1951), who may have shot more than a thousand elephants before World War I and is considered the most famous elephant hunter of all times. Of course he was hunting for a different purpose. He was doing it to earn money from ivory, in addition to liking the life he was leading. That was at the beginning of the twentieth century, when there was a great abundance of animals and no limits or sense that there was anything wrong in shooting great numbers of animals. In those times people thought the supply to be endless.

Nowadays this would not be thought of as hunting. Bell would be considered a killer overshooting just to get rich. But Karamojo Bell did it the hard way from a very modest beginning. They used to walk their feet off in those days. In one of his books he estimates that in his quest for ivory, between the years 1902 and 1907, he walked nearly 62,000 miles. His expeditions were sometimes made up of a hundred natives and their wives. The region he hunted was mainly in the Karamojo (mostly Turkana territory northwest of Lake Rudolf in Kenya and Uganda), and therefore the nickname. He took his first ivory when he was twenty-two years old.

Having become a blood brother of a native chief, Bell had the chief teach him where the elephant's relatively small brain is located by chopping open a skull. From then on he used only small-caliber rifles with which he shot elephants using very precise brain shots. Knowing where the brain was he could shoot an elephant with one clean shot, unlike so many other hunters who took many shots that only wounded the animal. This fact alone would have been sufficient to make him worthy of being highly considered in the history of hunting. Here was a great man who at the same time can be faulted when judged by modern hunting standards. But I always believe that one must never judge a person outside of his own context—in Bell's case, about a century ago.

Another famous man, also British, was Sir Samuel Baker (1821–93). Baker came from a rich family and had the strong-willed, independent character of an explorer-hunter of the early Victorian period. At twenty-two, together with his brother, he was sent by their father to manage the family plantation in Mauritius. They soon got bored there and went on to Ceylon, where they persuaded their father to buy an estate. Those were the days of black powder, and Baker used very heavy guns like the one specially made for him by Gibbs, the barrel of which was thirty-six inches long, with a powder charge one-third of the weight of the projectile. Later he added a four-bore percussion rifle weighing seventeen pounds made by Harris Holland, the founder of the famous firm.

With these guns he began shooting dangerous animals like elephant and water buffalo from close quarters, despising those that did so from a safer distance. Afterward he hunted stags, big boars, and leopard with hounds; once they were brought to bay, he would dispatch them with a hunting knife. On his return to Scotland he used the same method with red stags, amazing his companions. During his first years in Ceylon he shot many elephants, motivated by the government reward for elephants paid because of the damage they were causing to the plantations. He wrote some good books, interesting accounts of his hunting experiences.

After a time he himself evolved, and he began to think about animals and to learn to respect them, taking into account the sporting aspects of hunting. I find his writings interesting in that respect. He was a man that began just by shooting because it was fun and then came to know the animals and to respect them. This is one of the most interesting cases of the evolution of a hunter.

Women Hunters

As to women hunters, both in ancient and modern times there are some outstanding examples. Some, like Casey Schwabland and Ellen Enzler-Herring in our day, have also been writers. In fact, since 1995 the Safari Club International has established the Diana Award among its major prizes, honoring those women that have excelled in big-game hunting.

There were women hunter-explorers in the nineteenth century, extraordinary cases, who were not there as wives of their husbands but in their own right. Bartle Bull's book *Safari, a Chronicle of Adventure* has a chapter precisely on those women who went out exploring and hunting, and how the natives respected and helped them. As an example he mentions Mary Kingsley, who although more of a naturalist than a hunter went out in West Africa toward the end of the century in a heavy black skirt and tall, lace-up boots, preferring to walk or use a canoe as transport with a small party of native retainers. She died of enteric fever nursing prisoners during the Boer War.

A few years later, in 1907, the cousins Agnes and Cecily Herbert, in their early thirties, both very good shots, enjoyed more than four months' hunting in the bush of Somaliland. Dressed in knickerbockers, gaiters, shooting boots, and khaki safari jackets, they used as transport nearly fifty well-laden camels.

Those were not days when women usually did these sorts of things. These were exceptional women. I wouldn't say there were many, but there are cases of amazing, extraordinary women. Of course, there were also magnificent wives who accompanied their husbands, such as Florence Baker, who hunted with her husband, Sam, and Mary, Dr. David Livingstone's wife, who died of malaria on his first Zambezi expedition.

Final Message

As a final message to anybody interested in hunting, I would say that whatever you do in life, you must never shirk a challenge. And sometimes you must seek out challenges. I think that all men, each in his own sphere of life, should look for challenges. As Rudyard Kipling says in the well-known poem "If," listing manly attributes: "If you can be and do all these things, my boy, yours is the earth and everything that's in it and, which is more, you'll be a Man my son." Being a real hunter is being a man, in the most complete way, both spiritually and physically.

SAFARI PRESS